THERAPEUTIC PRINCIPLES IN SOCIAL WORK PRACTICE
A Primer for Clinicians

Herbert S. STREAN, D.S.W.

JASON ARONSON INC.
Northvale, New Jersey
London

THE MASTER WORK SERIES

Copyright © 1985 by Sage Publications, Inc.

New Printing 1993

Library of Congress Cataloging-in-Publication Data *pending*

ISBN: 1-56821-137-6

Manufactured in the United States of America. Jason Aronson Inc. offers books and cassettes. For information and catalog write to Jason Aronson Inc., 230 Livingston Street, Northvale, New Jersey 07647.

CONTENTS

To

Lyon P. Strean, Ph.D.
(1902-1964)

and

George J. Strean, M.D.
(1898-1971)

Principled Therapists

PREFACE

During the course of my work as a practitioner and teacher of psychotherapy, many students and colleagues have frequently expressed the need for a manual that would identify the major principles involved in doing effective therapeutic work. This book has been written to identify and discuss those principles that appear most pertinent in performing disciplined, effective, and humane therapeutic practice.

Over the years I have developed several convictions about the nature of therapeutic practice. One of these convictions is that it is extremely difficult for most people to ask for therapeutic help, very trying for them to participate in it, and most frightening for them to make interpersonal and intrapsychic changes. Although all of our clients consciously want to feel better and to function better, concomitantly they unconsciously champion the status quo, consistently distort the therapist's intentions, and frequently arrange to find obstacles to prevent them from maturing. I have never observed an adult client who in many ways did not show that he or she was unconsciously attempting to be a child.

Another conviction that has evolved during the course of my work is that those clinicians who fail to sensitize themselves to the fact that clients frequently respond to the therapist in many irrational ways and that they continually fight change, rarely achieve effective therapeutic results. Therefore, two dimensions of therapeutic life which I want to describe and clarify in this manual are transference (the client's idiosyncratic responses to the therapist) and resistance (the client's fighting against the therapeutic process).

Although often neglected in the social work and psychotherapeutic literature, another of the salient features of psychotherapy which I would like to discuss in this manual are the therapist's subjective reactions to the client, which always have an impact on the therapeutic outcome. Unless clinicians are aware of their countertransference responses, their work will tend to be hit or miss.

Students and practitioners who do therapeutic work are frequently overwhelmed by the vast array of theories and techniques that are at their disposal. As a result, they are extremely uncertain as to where they are going with their clients, why they are going there, and how to get there with them.

My desire in this manual is to make the underlying rationale of therapeutic work with clients as clear as possible. Whether the student or practitioner is working in a mental health center, a child guidance clinic, a family agency, a hospital, a private practice, or a public welfare setting, certain therapeutic principles are always germane to the clinical work. All clinicians must recognize that inherent in a client's presentation of problems are usually nonrational components and some distortions of reality. As mentioned, rare is the client who acts and feels like a mature adult all of the time. Therefore, all clinicians must differentiate between what clients desire from treatment and what they need from it. This will be discussed in detail in Chapter 1, "The Presenting Problem."

The dynamically oriented clinician should understand how every client in many ways is reliving his or her past in the present and distorting current relationships as if they were ones from childhood. Not only should the client's rational self and positive ego strengths be assessed comprehensively, but also clinicians should sensitize themselves to the irrational and illogical components that are always inherent in the client's functioning in and out of therapy. This will be discussed in considerable detail in Chapter 2, "The Psychosocial Assessment."

After the therapist has made a comprehensive psychosocial assessment of his or her client, he or she should formulate a therapeutic plan in which goals should be clearly explicated. By devising a sound therapeutic plan, the therapist can then appropriately choose a therapeutic modality—short-term treatment, family therapy, group treatment, and so on. This will be the topic of Chapter 3, "The Treatment Plan."

What most influences the outcome of any therapeutic experience is the therapist-client relationship. How the two parties experience each other will in many ways determine how the client accepts or rejects help and how much the client's psychosocial maturity will be enhanced. This extremely crucial dynamic component of therapy will be discussed in Chapter 4, "The Client-Therapist Relationship."

Very few texts in social work and psychotherapy specify which therapeutic procedures are most helpful for a particular client at a particular time. When is it helpful to make an interpretation? When is a confrontation more appropriate? Or a question? This issue will be discussed in Chapter 5, "Therapeutic Procedures." Of extreme pertinence in discussing therapeutic procedures is the client's response to them. Often, a therapist will make a statement that is intended to be supportive of the client but is experienced by the latter as an attack, responding in some way other than how the therapist intended. How do we account for this phenomenon, and what does the clinician do about it?

In Chapter 6, "Resistance and Counterresistance," we will consider a universal paradox of psychotherapy. All clients, despite their interpersonal and psychological pains and aches, resist change. Often, they consciously and deliberately want to defeat the therapist and render him or her impotent. Consequently, therapists need to sensitize themselves to the many direct and indirect ways in which clients sabotage treatment. They also need to utilize those therapeutic procedures which will most expediently help clients resolve their resistances. Further, all therapists need to be vigilant regarding how and when they, themselves, are resisting facing certain issues in the treatment—their clients' or their own anger, their clients' or their own sexual fantasies, and their clients' or their own anxieties.

In the final chapter, "Termination," we will discuss some of the features of the termination process in therapy and how to help client and therapist effect a meaningful and constructive separation.

The principles and procedures described in this manual are suitable for most clients in most settings. They have been used over and over again with many different kinds of people and with much success. What is extremely vital, as I have tried to demonstrate throughout this manual, is that interventive procedures should be adapted to the client and not the reverse. Individualization of the client is always extremely important regardless of setting or modality.

One of the most helpful aspects of this manual, in my opinion, is that every therapeutic principle is illuminated by a case example. The individuals and families described herein are real people, although identifying facts have been modified to respect confidentiality.

I would like to thank the many colleagues, students, teachers, and clients who have contributed ideas and case examples to this book. I would also like to express my gratitude to Professors Charles Garvin and Armand Lauffer of the University of Michigan's Graduate School of Social Work.

Chapter 1

THE PRESENTING PROBLEM

Only one-third of applicants to social agencies stay in treatment beyond the first interview (Strean, 1978; Perlman, 1968), and the number of dropouts in private practice is probably also quite high. While a large percentage of the individuals and families who are referred to or seek out social workers and other helping professionals are poorly motivated and are very frightened to accept help, many of these potential clients are capable of sustaining their contact with the practitioner if the latter can be sensitive to the latent messages that clients present in their early interviews. These messages, if listened to carefully, provide some understanding of the clients' discomforts about receiving help and some indication about their suspicions regarding the helper (Langs, 1981).

In this chapter, we will discuss some of the reasons that clients have difficulty in asking for therapeutic assistance, and we will present some case illustrations to illuminate this phenomenon. We will also try to demonstrate how the client's view of the agency and of the clinician is in many ways shaped by how the client experiences the referral process and the referral party.

The client's expectations of help and his or her fantasies about what will transpire with the therapist must be differentiated from what the client needs therapeutically; this issue will also be addressed in this chapter. Finally, we will discuss and show examples of some of the dynamics present in the client's first phone call and during the client's first interview. Our attempt throughout this chapter will be to demonstrate how the therapist can enhance or hinder the smooth flow of the initial stage of the helping process.

DIFFICULTIES IN ASKING FOR HELP

Whenever prospective clients are referred for therapeutic help or seek it out themselves, inevitably a part of them opposes it. Most individuals, despite their conscious recognition that all is not well in their interpersonal and psychic lives, experience therapeutic help as a blow to their narcissism and a puncturing of their self-esteem. Consequently, they view the person in the helping role with some caution and with some suspicion. Many applicants who seek therapeutic help do not become clients because the clinician failed to help them verbalize their discomfort about receiving therapeutic assistance. It is extremely important for the clinician to be vigilant with regard to the subtle ways clients can express their opposition to becoming the recipients of professional counsel.

Barbara and Al Adams, a couple in their early thirties, were referred to a family agency for marriage counseling. Although they both spoke easily about their marital arguments and their anxiety and doubt about themselves and each other, when the interview was near termination, Barbara asked the social worker, "Do many people in our circumstances need this sort of stuff?" The social worker, Mr. Z, attempting to reassure the Adamses, said, "It is a very common occurrence." While Barbara and Al nodded and went on to make an appointment for a second visit to see Mr. Z, they never showed up for the appointment and could not be persuaded to return for more help.

It became clear to Ms. Y, a social worker at another agency whom the Adamses saw two months after they had seen Mr. Z, that Barbara's question concerning the number of people who need marriage counseling was a subtle expression of her doubts about receiving help and an indication of her feelings of vulnerability in the therapeutic setting. When the same question was asked by Barbara of Ms. Y, Ms. Y asked the Adamses, "Perhaps you feel somewhat uncomfortable about going ahead with this?" Both the Adamses talked about feeling "inadequate" in not being able to take care of their problems by themselves, expressed the notion that they felt like children, and did not like the idea of "being under someone else's guidance." The Adamses then again mentioned their contact with Mr. Z and said that they did not believe him when he said that marital conflict and marriage counseling were common occurrences.

Barbara and Al needed several interviews with Ms. Y to discuss their discomfort before they could move into the counseling situation and participate in it with some degree of comfort.

Many beginning therapists and even some experienced ones often appear too eager to begin treatment without allowing their clients an opportunity to discuss their anxiety about being in it. Sometimes a discussion of their anxiety can take four, five, or more interviews, but these interviews are absolutely necessary if the helping process is to be successful. Not only do prospective clients feel more trusting of the helper and of the helping process if the professional recognizes their doubts and vulnerabilities, and not only are they more willing to participate in the helping process if they feel understood, but of tremendous importance is the fact that prospective clients begin to understand themselves better and begin to function better when their doubts about treatment are addressed by the helper.

Jack Broad, a man in his forties, had been fired from several jobs. In addition to his frequent fracases with his employers and colleagues, he suffered from alcoholism. When he was referred for counseling by his physician, he seemed to comply and made an appointment to see Mr. W, a social worker.

After telling Mr. W about his problems, Jack said, "I found this conversation helpful. I think I can make it alone, now." Mr. W, aware that Jack was experiencing some doubts about further help, said, "You'd rather help yourself without my assistance. How come?" Jack was then able to talk about distrusting anybody who was eager to help him, how he felt that nobody really cared about him, and that he got more gratification from drinking than from any human relationship.

As Jack and Mr. W talked more and more about how the client distrusted his helper, he was able to get in touch with a great deal of anger that he harbored toward his parents, whom he described as "undependable." Feeling accepted by Mr. W while he vented anger at his parents and discharged some irritation at Mr. W, Jack said, in his seventh interview, "Since I've been talking to you, I feel more energy. I think that all that anger we've been talking about sapped my energy and made me more distrustful than I've had to be."

When clients show their distrust of the helping process, it is tempting for the helper to offer reassuring statements, give promises that beneficial results will accrue from the help, or even go so far as to intervene prematurely in their clients' environment. This frequently happens with clients in public assistance programs who, although very needy, are also very suspicious of those who want to assist them. Unless the caseworker discusses with these clients how uncomfortable they feel when they are being helped, the clients become "dropouts." Reassurance rarely helps suspicious and distrustful clients modify their doubts. Rather, such clients need an opportunity to discuss their questions about treatment with a benign, quiet listener.

> Ms. Sally Cunningham, age 22, was a single parent of three children and had many difficulties—financial, health, interpersonal, and legal. When she told her caseworker in her second interview that she had a great deal of difficulty coping with her landlord, her caseworker, Ms. V, said that she would speak to Ms. Cunningham's landlord for her. Ms. Cunningham responded with, "Good, I can't do it myself." Feeling that her client was most receptive to her offer of help with the landlord, Ms V then told Ms. Cunningham that she would tell her about the results of her interview with the landlord at their next appointment. However, Ms. Cunningham did not show up for her next appointment or the one after that.

> Perplexed, Ms. V decided to make a home visit and try to ascertain what was transpiring between her and her client. After some protests and denials, Ms. Cunningham, a black woman, was able to say to Ms. V, "To tell you the truth I don't trust white women. They smile at you but they feel holier than you. I feel like a second-class citizen next to you." Ms. V, now sensitive to the fact that her client felt very ambivalent about being a recipient of her assistance, told Ms. Cunningham that she guessed she had moved too fast in trying to help her and had not spent enough time talking to her about how difficult it was to accept her help. Feeling more understood and more accepted, Ms. Cunningham could then spend several interviews with Ms. V discussing how weak and inferior she felt next to Ms. V.

> It was only after several interviews in which she discussed her ambivalence about being helped that Ms. Cunningham could consider accepting some assistance.

Helping professionals need to recognize that every client has doubts and anxieties about being helped and that these doubts and anxieties need to be aired, not circumvented or shoved under a rug. An old axiom from social work states, "Begin where the client is" (Hamilton, 1951). This mandate implies that before clients are given concrete services and/or therapeutic help, they frequently need to talk about what it feels like to sit across the desk and be a client. This is where many clients are at the beginning of the helping process.

As clients initiate treatment, they are frequently worried that they will be punished for their aggression, entrapped for their sexual wishes, demeaned for their dependency, or scoffed at for their childishness. Individuals who resist beginning therapy often point out, "It is an invasion of my privacy," and they tend to view the therapist as a cruel voyeur rather than as an enhancing enabler (Strean, 1985).

While the mental health of individuals in psychotherapy is the same or possibly a little better than those who are not in treatment, because individuals in psychotherapy are not as plagued by denial and have more courage to face themselves (Fine, 1982), it is still the rare individual who does not experience going into treatment as some kind of failure. "When I think of depending on a therapist, I feel like a fool for not being able to take care of myself," stated an applicant at a family agency. "If I were a mature parent, I would not have to come to a child guidance clinic for help," said a dejected father at intake. Remarked a man whose wife suggested that he consider treatment at a mental health center for his depression, "I'll be damned if I'm going to pull down my pants for a stranger." All of these comments attest to the fact that being the recipient of therapeutic help conjures up painful associations and anxious thoughts.

THE CLIENT'S ATTITUDE TOWARD
THE REFERRAL PARTY

While clients often seek out treatment at their own behest, more frequently they are referred by others, such as ministers, judges, physicians, attorneys, family, and friends. What is often overlooked by intake workers and other clinicians is that the way clients feel toward the referring source will greatly influence how they will relate to the therapist. If a client feels ambivalent toward the physician who referred him, inevitably he will be ambivalent toward the clinician. If a client feels hostile toward the judge who forced him to go into treatment or else threatened him with jail, then the practitioner who greets this client will, sooner or later, be the recipient of much hostility.

Sgt. Neil Davis, a career soldier 43 years of age who had been in the military for more than fifteen years, was seen in the medical dispensary of his army post by a physician who diagnosed his condition of *pruritis ani* (itchy anus) as psychosomatic and referred him to the post's mental hygiene clinic. Inasmuch as the physician was a colonel, Sgt. Davis felt intimidated by him and complied with his recommendation.

At the mental hygiene clinic, Sgt. Davis had his first appointment with Lt. U. Before the latter sat down, Sgt. Davis attacked him and told Lt. U that he, Lt. U, was "crazy." Feeling somewhat surprised, Lt. U asked, "What's upsetting you so much?" Sgt. Davis then had a powerful temper tantrum and condemned physicians, social workers, the mental hygiene movement, and eventually the whole army medical corps. Pointing angrily to his anus, he shouted, "It hurts here!" and pointing to his head, he shouted again, "Not there!" He felt it was absolutely ridiculous for the "stupid colonel" to send him "to get my head examined when something else needs attention."

Lt. U told Sgt. Davis that he could now understand what upset him so much. Stated Lt. U, "You feel you don't belong here! You feel you've been sent to the wrong place." Feeling a bit better understood, Sgt. Davis could more easily talk about his life circumstances, his marital problems, and other "pains." However, it took him more than five interviews before he could lessen his outrage toward the physician who referred him, and at least ten interviews before he could become more trusting of Lt. U.

Often when prospective clients are referred to therapists by judges, attorneys, or other figures of authority, they are told that if they do not accept the referral, the consequences will be quite severe. Imprisonment, divorce, and suspension from school are some of the threats given. Inasmuch as these alternatives to treatment appear so ominous, many prospective clients accept treatment, albeit reluctantly.

It should come as no surprise to the helping practitioner that prospective clients who are involuntarily referred for treatment often have a strong antipathy toward it. Feeling coerced, they experience therapy as something akin to a concentration camp and react to it with either fury or depression. Because the involuntary client hates the idea of treatment but often cannot tell anybody this, the sensitive clinician knows that unless the client's resentment is faced and discharged in the therapist's office, treatment will have a limited effect or none at all (Blanck & Blanck, 1974). This is a difficult process for both client and practitioner to confront, because to the client, the therapist often appears similar to the coercive judge, the authoritarian school official, or the threatening lover or spouse, and many therapists feel uncomfortable being cast into these roles.

With an involuntary client, two important issues must be considered before treatment can get off the ground: First, the practitioner must try to help the client discharge his fury about being in the therapeutic situation; second, the practitioner must try to help the client eventually recognize that the helping person is not the same person who referred the client for treatment.

Shirley Graham, age 14, was referred to a mental hygiene clinic because she had been truant from school. Her principal at the school took the position that either she enter treatment or she would be sent to "a reformatory for wayward girls."

When Shirley greeted the social worker, Ms. T, she immediately blurted out, "I don't want to be here, I've been forced to be here." Recognizing that Shirley was transferring onto her all the characteristics of the authoritarian principal who referred her for treatment, Ms. T said, "I don't blame you for not wanting to be here if you've been forced to come." Surprised at Ms. T's accepting and noncritical reaction, Shirley said, "You are darn right. I will never do anything I'm forced to do." Again, Ms. T tried to be empathetic and said, "This stuff never works when somebody feels forced."

Shirley went on to tell Ms. T that all her life she had been told what to do. "My parents think they are gods, my teacher thinks he's Napoleon, and the principal thinks he's a king. I'm sick and tired of taking orders and I'm not going to be ordered to come here." After a moment or two of silence, Shirley went on to say, "If I don't come here, I'll land up at that place for crazy kids and that's worse. So I better come here." Ms. T remarked, "I know you don't want to go to the reformatory, but seeing me is no bargain either." Shirley laughed and said, "Maybe I'll come here if you don't tell me what to do when I'm here." Ms. T laughed and said, "Maybe you can tell me what to do if you do decide to come here for a while." Shirley said that she liked Ms. T and was grateful for her "attitude." She suggested that she would come to see Ms. T if they did not talk about "psychological stuff." Maybe they could talk about the New York Yankees baseball team or discuss some of the latest movies.

Ms. T tried to adapt to Shirley's prescription. Discussion of the Yankees "being in the cellar" and consideration of movies in which the leading actor or actress was being scapegoated eventually led to an examination of Shirley's real problems. Feeling genuinely understood and accepted for herself, Shirley could move toward trusting her helper with some degree of confidence and eventually looked at how she felt "in the cellar" and how she felt she was being scapegoated.

Involuntary clients are usually individuals who feel very controlled and dominated. If they are given the feeling that treatment is a voluntary process and are convinced that the therapist really believes this and that he or she will not impose anything on them, these clients often become more accepting of a therapeutic relationship. Furthermore, as was true in the case of Shirley, if these clients are afforded the opportunity to contribute to the therapeutic agenda, they usually feel less coerced and freer to relate to the therapist.

Inasmuch as the involuntary client frequently appears very belligerent toward the therapist and very rejecting of any attempt on his or her part to offer help, this client is quite capable of inducing strong countertransference reactions in the helper. Practitioners, in response to the involuntary client's contempt, can react in kind (Schafer, 1983) and can become contemptuous of the client, however subtly. Some therapists even provide a therapeutic rationale for their contempt (Spotnitz, 1976) and point out that the hostile client "needs" hostile therapeutic responses. However, this kind of reaction on the therapist's part only convinces involuntary clients that helping professionals cannot be trusted, and they become concerned with the idea that the therapist cannot cope with what really ails them.

Jerry Frank, age 45, was referred to a social worker by his wife, Dot, who threatened him with divorce unless he got therapeutic assistance for his sexual problems. Dot was "fed up" with his disinterest in sex and with his sexual impotence, which had existed for several years. Although Jerry and Dot had many arguments about their sexual life and also about therapy, Jerry seemed to feel that Dot was serious about leaving him and therefore sought treatment.

After Jerry told Mr. S, his social worker, that he was not "turned on" by Dot and therefore did not have much interest in her sexually, he then suggested that Dot was really the one who needed treatment because "she's a bitch." Failing to understand how vulnerable Jerry was feeling in the interview, and unaware that he was on the attack because he felt attacked, Mr. S felt frustrated by Jerry's attitude. Instead of letting him attack Dot, and in lieu of hearing about his reluctance to go into therapy, Mr. S subtly provoked Jerry. He told him that he seemed to have conflicts of his own and was more interested to talk about Dot than he was interested in looking at himself. Feeling put on the spot by Mr. S, Jerry tried to put Mr. S on the spot by asking him, "What are *your* sexual problems like?" When Mr. S asked Jerry why he asked, Jerry told Mr. S he was "a dodger" and was "afraid to reveal himself."

While Mr. S was correct in his analysis that Jerry was projecting his own wish to evade onto others, Jerry was far from ready to hear this.

Furthermore, Mr. S was using his interpretive know-how to attack Jerry rather than to help him understand himself better. Feeling misunderstood and unsupported, Jerry decided to have nothing further to do with Mr. S and left the interview before it was formally terminated, never to return again.

When clients, voluntary or involuntary, project their difficulties onto their spouses and/or onto the therapist, it is helpful to these clients to let them continue to project. As they subject the therapist or the spouse to examination and are not attacked for this, they may become freer to look at these qualities in themselves.

Practitioners can come to feel less attacked and less threatened by the involuntary client by reminding themselves periodically that this client's belligerence masks feelings of desperation, terror, and weakness. To defend against the panic that evolves from deep feelings of unworthiness, the client provokes the therapist so that the latter will feel what the client is trying to deny: the unpleasant feelings of inadequacy and despair.

While the prognosis for a client's success in treatment is much better when he has been referred by someone toward whom he feels positive, there are some cautions that have to be observed when this is the case. Often the client very much idealizes the referral party. For example, a minister, physician, or friend can be so admired by the client that he or she is ready to expect the helper to be full of omnipotent qualities that will lead the client to the "promised land."

Just as it is important for the practitioner to help the applicant see differences between the therapist and a referral party toward whom the applicant feels hostile, it is equally crucial for the practitioner to help an individual begin to appreciate that the former is not an omnipotent and magical god who can work wonders in a few minutes. If this is not done, the client will soon become disillusioned and leave treatment.

The Eaton family was referred to a family therapist, Mr. R, by their minister, because Mr. and Mrs. Eaton and their son and daughter were frequently arguing with one another and quite intensely. The minister, Rev. A, was highly esteemed by all of the family members, and they referred to him affectionately as "Grandpa." When the Eatons were advised by Rev. A that they needed family counseling, they quickly took his advice because all of them agreed, "Grandpa knows best."

In their initial consultation with Mr. R, the Eatons told him that they were very pleased to meet him because Rev. A had recommended him so highly. Furthermore, if Mr. R was a colleague of Rev. A, he had to be "terrific." Feeling flattered by the Eatons' appraisal of him, Mr. R basked in the glow of their compliments. He was so appreciative of their flattery that he did not, at any point, explore their family problems.

The Eatons returned for two more family sessions and continued to flatter both Rev. A and Mr. R. However, by the fourth session, all of the Eatons seemed quite subdued. When Mr. R called their quiet and inhibited demeanor to their attention, exploration revealed that the family had been very disappointed with Mr. R. Said Mr. Eaton, "We thought that things would be much better now, but they aren't," and the other family members agreed with him. Fortunately, Mr. R was able to recognize that the Eatons were expecting some kind of magical relief, and he used his understanding to help them. He said, "Rev. A is very highly regarded by you and he spoke highly of me. I guess you felt I would be able to help you much more than I have in these last three interviews." Feeling a bit more understood now, the Eatons acknowledged their very high expectations of Mr. R, revealed their anger toward him, and were eventually able to see that they would have to examine their family conflicts in therapy before any major changes could take place. Interestingly, one of the major problems of the Eatons was their very high and unrealistic expectations of themselves and of each other. It took them several months before they could accept the fact that Mr. R, Rev. A, and they, themselves, were all human beings who, because they were human, were individuals with limitations and imperfections.

How the referring party defines a problem will be very important in helping potential clients adapt to the therapeutic situation. A minister might tell a member of his congregation that he or she needs group therapy; a group might be advised by a lawyer that they need an advocate or a social broker; an organization might be informed by a civil rights leader that they need new social utilities. The sensitive practitioner always recognizes that referral parties are often expressing their own biases and unrealistic fantasies in assessing a client's needs; their assessments may or may not be in the client's best interests. Furthermore, if clients are feeling positively toward the referral party, they will be inclined to endorse the referral party's prescription; if they are having negative thoughts toward the referral party, they will probably oppose the recommendations, and if they are feeling ambivalent, they will, in all likelihood, feel mixed about the referral party's suggestions.

Regardless of how the client is feeling toward the referral party and toward the latter's definition of the problem, this issue must be carefully explored.

Lloyd Harrington, age 37, was referred by his wife to a family agency for "sexual counseling." In the opening minutes of his first interview with the social worker, Ms. Q, Lloyd said, "I'm sexually impotent and have very serious sexual problems. I need help immediately or my marriage will go down the drain!" When Ms. Q asked Lloyd what happened between him and his wife sexually, Lloyd apologetically brought out the following: "I frequently have to kiss my wife, fondle her, and be fondled by her before I can have an erection. This usually takes from five to seven minutes and this gets my wife angry and frantic. She rebukes me for my slowness, and then I get angry at her and my erection gets further delayed."

As Ms. Q explored Lloyd's sexual difficulties, she discovered that Lloyd was a man who tended to acquiesce to almost everybody's demands. He could like himself only if he felt he was pleasing the other person, and he frequently hated himself when he felt or was told that he was not satisfying someone else. Consequently, Ms. Q shared her observation about Lloyd's compliance with him and said, "Your coming to see me seems to be out of a desire to please your wife more than anything else." Lloyd agreed, but insightfully stated, "Maybe what I should come to see you for is to find out why I have to be a puppy-dog for everybody and please all of my masters."

As we have reiterated, the client frequently relates to the social worker in the same way he does to the referral party, as was true in the above case. Lloyd Harrington was a man who was inclined to be obedient and submissive. This was the way he related to his wife. He compliantly accepted her prescriptions for treatment and was ready to turn the therapist into his master. If Ms. Q had not called this coping mechanism of Lloyd's to his attention, treatment might have been reduced to another "dog-master" relationship, which would have been unproductive.

Reactions to the referral party give clues to the client's wishes, fears, anxieties, and defenses. If clients are submissive or ambivalent or hostile toward the referring party, they are indirectly suggesting how they tend to cope with interpersonal relationships in general. What coping and defense mechanisms, anxieties, strengths, and vulnerabilities are at work when a client responds to a referral party will all become a part of the therapist's assessment and interventive treatment plan (Strean, 1978).

DIFFERENTIATING CLIENT REQUESTS FROM
THE CLIENT'S THERAPEUTIC NEEDS

Most people, by the time they seek help from a social worker or from some other helping professional, are quite desperate. Seeking therapeutic assistance, as we have already noted, often implies to them that they are weak and failing. Clients rarely recognize that it is the strong who come for help and it is the courageous who are willing to face themselves. In our culture, denial of problems is subtly championed, and facing psychological and interpersonal conflicts is often repudiated. Consequently, the anxiety that clients feel when they come for help is usually quite high, and, because of this, they cannot see their problems clearly or talk about them lucidly.

Usually, a client's simple request is a disguised cry for help in dealing with more complex conflicts. For example, a woman who comes to a social agency with a request for divorce counseling may really be more interested in exploring her hatred and her ambivalence toward her husband. A couple who request guidance in handling their child may need some help with their marital conflicts. A family that requests help from a lawyer may need help with their interpersonal relationships.

Clients' requests from the practitioner may be viewed, in certain respects, as dreams; they have both manifest and latent content. Just as a person who has a simple dream of eating a steak, upon associating to the dream, may learn that he has more complex and conflicting desires which are symbolized by the steak, a client's simple request for job counseling, for divorce mediation, or for placement of a child, upon careful exploration by the practitioner, may reveal more complex needs and more complex conflicts. The following vignettes illustrate the point that all client requests need to be fully investigated.

Marilyn and David Ingersoll, a couple in their early thirties, came to a child guidance clinic because their son, Jack, age 6, suffered from insomnia. As they discussed the details of Jack's sleeping difficulties with Mr. P, the intake worker, it turned out that Jack slept in the parental bedroom with his parents. When the sleeping arrangements were further investigated, what emerged was that the Ingersolls had acute sexual difficulties and that was what became the focus of their treatment.

Sarah Joseph, a single woman in her early twenties, applied to the local community center because she was interested in joining The Singles Group—a group of young people between the ages of 18 and 25 that met weekly for dancing, discussions, and theater parties. When Ms. O, the social worker, asked Sarah what she was hoping to get out of the experience with The Singles Group, Sarah began to cry and talked of a deep depression that she had been experiencing for the last several months. Although Sarah did eventually participate in The Singles Group, she needed intensive psychotherapy before she could feel comfortable in group situations. Her request to join The Singles Group was a disguised cry for therapeutic help to deal with her depression and social anxiety.

Jane and Leon Kaplan, a couple in their late thirties, told the social worker at the family agency that they wanted to place their 10-year-old son in an institution. According to the Kaplans, their son, Peter, was "murderous, impulsive, and had no conscience." Further exploration of Peter's difficulties and a closer investigation of Jane and Leon's relationship with Peter revealed that the former were extremely terrified of their own murderous impulses and were extremely worried that they might destroy Peter impulsively. Jane commented after their second interview with the social worker, Mr. N, "We thought we'd be helped to get rid of him [Peter]; instead, we are going to come here to find out why we want to kill him."

The requests clients make of practitioners are as varied as the person-situation constellations of the clients themselves. Because of their acute anxiety, they often ask the helping professional for permission to behave in a certain way—or for a warning, a limit, protection, or a combination of these things. Every client's request, no matter how farfetched, needs to be heard in all its details and explored further.

Inexperienced social workers and other clinicians who have not been sufficiently sensitized to the many complexities of the helping process frequently fail to differentiate between a client's request and his or her therapeutic needs. They are insufficiently aware that it is very difficult for many clients to articulate their problems clearly and that in many cases, clients need much time and attention before they can be sure of what they really need from a helping professional.

THE FIRST PHONE CALL

Usually a client first requests help from an agency, treatment center, or private practitioner by making a phone call. It is important to keep in mind that most prospective clients have postponed making the phone call for weeks, months, and, in some cases, years. As we have already implied, calling someone up for therapeutic help can be frightening, anxiety-provoking, and often is dreaded. Consequently, the practitioner should be aware that when prospective clients ask questions over the phone about fees, frequency of interviews, theoretical predilections of the therapist, and so forth, they are often masking their fears and are trying to cope with their doubts.

Some candidates for psychotherapy, because of their enormous anxiety about being trapped in a situation that appears overwhelming to them, secretly hope that the clinician will say or do something over the phone that will make entering treatment appear to be an incorrect move. They may hope that the therapist does not have time available for them, charges too high a fee, or has an orientation to treatment that appears incompatible with their own modus vivendi.

Because questions from the prospective client that are asked over the phone frequently emanate from his or her dread of involvement in treatment, direct answers from the practitioner can frequently compound the client's resistance to further help. For example, if a prospective client has fears of interpersonal closeness and asks over the phone if the agency (or practitioner) is Rogerian or Jungian, and the practitioner states the agency's orientation, the client's dread of treatment can be exacerbated. If the client wants a Rogerian therapist, and the therapist says over the phone that he is indeed a Rogerian, the client who is afraid of intimacy will have to find another reason to avoid the treatment. On the other hand, if the practitioner acknowledges that he is not Rogerian, then the prospective client has a good reason to resist the therapy and the therapist, because as far as the client is concerned, his needs are not being met.

Although beginning therapists feel very self-conscious when they do so, it is best to tell prospective clients that their questions regarding fees, frequency of appointments, theoretical orientations, and the like are important ones but that they are best discussed in the office. Neophyte therapists sometimes do not realize that most prospective clients welcome an approach that says implicitly, "I know you have all kinds of doubts, questions, and concerns. Come in and see me, maybe I can help you." If prospective clients cannot cope with the delay, in all probability their motivation for help is quite weak and their terror of it is quite strong. This frequently becomes apparent over the phone.

Norman Landy, a man in his late twenties, called Ms. M, a social worker in private practice for help in "learning how to get along better with women." Over the phone, Norman asked Ms. M, "Are you one of the Freudian types?" When Ms. M said, "Why don't you come in and we can discuss it?" Norman insisted on getting an answer and said, "I have to know before I come in whether you are Freudian or not!" When Ms. M asked Norman what his concern was all about, Norman responded, "I don't want to be pushed into having sex, and Freudians do that!" After a silence, Norman asked, "Will you push me into having sex?" Ms. M then said, "I am wondering if you are a man who is very worried about being pushed around by women. Maybe you'd like to wait a while before you come to see me." Feeling freer, Norman did come in for a consultation and spent some time in treatment exploring his fear of having women dominate him and order him about.

Prospective clients are quite suspicious of practitioners who are eager to push them into treatment. They wonder if the practitioners are "money-hungry" or suffer from some other interpersonal problem.

Rachel Miller, a young woman in her twenties, called Dr. N for a consultation. Over the phone, Rachel told Dr. N, "I'm looking for someone who will be active and give me some feedback." Dr. N responded, "I'm a very active therapist. I don't believe in being passive." Rachel told Dr. N that she liked his attitude and made an appointment to see him. However, she never kept her appointment.

Several months later, Rachel called another therapist, Ms. L. On being asked over the phone whether she would be active and provide some feedback, Ms L suggested that Rachel might consider coming in for a consultation with her and discuss her concerns about the therapist's activity. Rachel kept her appointment and stayed in treatment with Ms. L.

Several weeks after Rachel had been in treatment with Ms. L, she explained why she responded so negatively to Dr. N. "He seemed too eager to have me work with him, and I became so suspicious of someone who was so eager. I wondered if he was in need of clients. He wanted too much too soon."

Sometimes requests made over the phone by prospective clients seem bizarre. However, every request has psychological meaning and should be explored in the practitioner's office. When requests of prospective clients conflict with the practitioner's habitual routines in conducting treatment, although there is a tendency to reject these requests, rejection never helped anybody. For example, a prospective client can call an agency, clinic, or private practitioner and ask for nude marathons, monthly therapy, or sexual encounter groups. Inexperienced and insensitive therapists can often dismiss these requests without giving full attention to the person asking them.

Bob North, a man in his forties, called a social agency because he wanted some help in finding a mate. He was not particularly interested in marrying the mate, but he wanted somebody with whom he could "have sex on a consistent basis." When the social worker on intake told Bob over the phone that the agency did not provide the service in which he was interested, Bob said, "You are a very officious woman and I would not want to meet you anywhere."

Several months after this telephone contact, Bob called Ms. K, a private practitioner. When Bob repeated the requests he had made of the agency, Ms. K asked him if he would like to come in and see her at her office and discuss his requests further. Bob responded positively to Ms. K's suggestion that he make an appointment.

During his initial consultation, Bob told Ms. K that he was an extremely lonely man who had not had a date with a woman in years. He talked about how socially inept he felt and how prone he was to anticipate rejection from people, particularly from women. He revealed a long and painful history of "never making it with anybody—at school, on the job, or anywhere." On Ms. K's suggesting that Bob come in to see her for another appointment, Bob readily complied.

When clients call therapists and make unusual requests, practitioners should keep in mind that clients are coping with life in the best possible way they know how, and that they need understanding and empathy from the practitioner. All too often therapists do not sufficiently respect a client's reluctance to get involved in treatment and try to bypass it by telling the prospective client over the phone to do something about his behavior immediately.

Henry Olsen, a man in his forties, at the urging of his wife, called Mr. J for treatment. When Mr. J heard that Henry wanted treatment every other week—that is, once every two weeks—Mr. J said over the phone, "If you want to get something out of it, you should come more often." Although Henry made an appointment with Mr. J, he never kept it. He told the person who ended up being his therapist that he felt much too pressured by Mr. J.

Virtually all applicants of psychotherapy protect themselves from imaginary or real danger. When practitioners sensitize themselves to this universal occurrence, they can better meet prospective clients where they are (Hamilton, 1951) and will not impose their own ways of coping on them.

Many candidates for treatment are very distrustful of their potential helpers, and their distrust must be honored, not refuted. Frequently, their distrust may take the form of not wanting to give the therapist information over the phone, as in the following case illustration (abridged from Strean, 1984):

> Herman P, a married man in his thirties, wanted job counseling and needed treatment for a variety of problems—depression, anxiety attacks, and physical symptoms. However, over the phone he would not give the prospective therapist his name. When the therapist, Dr. A, did not insist that Herman give his name but did offer him an appointment, Herman sounded quite relieved. He kept his appointment but continued to be very skeptical of the therapist and of the therapy for some time.

A difficult call for the practitioner to cope with is from the individual who is calling on behalf of a prospective client. Often a husband phones a therapist to arrange treatment for his wife, and just as frequently, a wife calls to arrange treatment for her husband. If the therapist asks the person who makes the phone call to arrange for the spouse to contact the agency, often the spouse is never heard from. Furthermore, when an appointment is made by one person for another, the appointment is broken by the prospective client.

Very frequently, when one person calls an agency or therapist for another, the individual calling is unconsciously asking for help for himself or herself. Most of the time, the parent, spouse, or friend who calls for someone else does not feel free to ask directly for treatment and finds it easier to ask for help for someone else. Yet if the caller's wish is interpreted over the phone and the caller is told that he or she wants treatment, the caller will probably deny it. Therefore, to respect the caller's latent wish for help and concomitantly respond to his or her resistance to treatment, the sensitive therapist will ask the individual making the phone call to come in and discuss his or her child's, spouse's, or friend's problem. Particularly parents and frequently spouses welcome the possibility of an appointment for such purposes. It should be mentioned that if phone callers do not want appointments for themselves, they usually do arrange for their spouse, friend, or colleague to call on their own. However, it should always be kept in mind that if one asks for help for someone else, he or she often wants it for himself or herself.

Jack W, age 36, called a mental health clinic to arrange treatment for his 12-year-old nephew, Mike. Over the phone he pointed out that Mike had difficulty forming relationships with peers, was truant from school, and felt hated by his parents. Stated Jack, "He needs to see someone quite soon," and seemed to imply that the situation was quite urgent. The attentive social worker, Ms. B, told Jack that she would like to discuss Jack's concerns about Mike, and suggested that he come in for an interview.

For the first few sessions, Jack talked exclusively about his nephew. Later, the discussion turned to how Jack had been "a substitute father" for Mike. While talking about being a father figure, Jack became quite teary and told Ms. B, the social worker, "I guess I'm giving Mike what I always wanted—a good father." Jack soon became a client in his own right and used his time with Ms. B to discuss his own problems. Several months later, he helped Mike call for his own appointment to be helped therapeutically.

Sooner or later, every clinician makes an appointment with a prospective client who does not show up for the interview. In most cases a canceled appointment is an indication that the applicant is frightened of what he fantasies will take place in the interview with the therapist. However, the nature of the prospective client's anxiety is usually very vague, and therefore it is difficult for most clinicians to relate to it. Sometimes the prospective client wants simply to feel wanted, and a telephone call rearranging the missed interview will suffice. In other instances, the reasons for the cancellation are more complicated. In almost every situation, however, the therapist should make an attempt to call the prospective client and see if his or her fear of treatment can be dealt with over the phone.

Most prospective clients respond positively when a therapist is not critical of them for not showing up for the initial interview. Even if it appears to be a rationalization, the client's manifest statement regarding his cancellation should be respected. Sometimes illnesses do intervene, accidents really do take place, and traffic snarls do occur. What is helpful for the prospective client who is frightened to be involved in treatment is a therapist who is accepting and not critical, understanding and nonjudgmental. Therefore, when a client cancels an appointment, the client should be told that it was regrettable that the interview could not take place and that another interview can be arranged.

When clients cancel more than one appointment, it is usually an indication of a real dread of treatment. All too often, therapists try to convince reluctant clients to come in for an interview. This stance bypasses the client's distrust and usually exacerbates his suspiciousness. Reluctant clients need to feel that they have the right to resist treatment. Sometimes therapists need to permit themselves and their reluctant clients several phone calls, often with much time intervening between the calls, before frightened clients can keep their appointments. Very frequently, when the therapist compassionately notes that beginning treatment might be something that the person would prefer to avoid right now, this attitude often frees the reluctant applicant to view therapy more favorably.

Patricia Rogers, a young woman of 19, had been referred to the college counseling service by her adviser. Patricia did not show up for four appointments and did not call to cancel them. When Ms. I, the social worker, phoned Patricia to make other appointments, Patricia pointed out that she either had forgotten about them or that she had been sick.

After Patricia canceled her fourth appointment, Ms. I told her over the phone that she had the impression that coming to see her was not a very welcome idea to Patricia and that perhaps she was thinking of not starting therapy right away. Patricia replied, "I really *must* come!" Here, Ms. I said, "Maybe that has something to do with it. You *must* come and perhaps it isn't comfortable to do things that you feel you *must* do." Patricia responded with laughter and said, "I think you know your business," and did come in for an appointment. She used her appointment with Ms. I to discuss how frequently she felt "pushed around," "controlled" and that everybody "demanded" so much of her.

From the moment an applicant for professional help initiates a phone call until the end of the phone conversation, the therapist realizes that the prospective client has many mixed feelings about calling, fears future contacts, and in many ways would prefer not to be on the telephone asking for an appointment. Consequently, the sensitive, empathic therapist tries to make it as safe as possible for the applicant by showing, through his or her behavior, that apprehension about the first interview is to be expected.

THE FIRST INTERVIEW

Most people who become clients do so because there is no one in their immediate environment to hear them out, and most listeners, when hearing someone describe an interpersonal or psychological problem, feel obliged to give advice, offering experiences of their own, or else they just feel helpless. They fail to recognize that one of the most effective ways of being helpful to someone in distress is to permit the interviewee plenty of latitude in voicing what is on his or on her mind (Barbara, 1958).

It frequently takes many years of experience for practitioners to accept the notion that a good interviewer is a good listener. Most practitioners incorrectly believe that a good interviewer talks a great deal and shows empathy by offering interpretations, presenting clarifications, and posing questions. They fail to grasp one of the most essential principles of therapy, which is that when an individual is given the opportunity to have a concerned listener attend to his or her thoughts, feelings, ideas, and memories, tensions are reduced and energy previously used to suppress disturbing feelings and thoughts becomes available for more productive living.

Every therapist learns that regardless of how miserable a client feels, the idea of changing his or her attitudes usually evokes a great deal of anxiety. The practitioner should try to permit the client as much opportunity as possible to talk about the many facets of his or her problems and examine alternatives. Inexperienced practitioners, in their zeal to ameliorate a client's distress, too often rush to solutions without obtaining a clear understanding of the individual's dynamics and an understanding of the complexities of his or her situation. To advise a marital couple to stay together or to separate without first making a comprehensive assessment of their personalities, interactions, loves, hates, and ambivalences can only intensify their distress. To advise a student to drop out or stay in school without first obtaining knowledge of his or her interests, conflicts, and anxieties will not help him or her. To prescribe a course of action prematurely before letting clients talk about the many sides of their problems is to squelch and control them. Clients resent overactive practitioners. They welcome helpers who quietly listen with interest.

The value of attentive listening may be seen from the following interview between an 11-year-old boy and the social worker at a therapeutic camp for emotionally disturbed youngsters.

> Bill's counselor brought him to the social worker, Mr. H, because after a few days of camp, Bill was not participating in any of the activities, was not eating or sleeping well, and appeared very depressed.

When Mr. H sat down with Bill, there was an initial silence. Mr. H then said, "You seem quite unhappy here. Would you like to talk about it?" At first Bill was reluctant to talk, but then he said that he did not like the camp, hated the kids, abhorred the activities, and wanted to be home. "At home everybody likes me; here nobody does," Bill stated vehemently. He went on to say that his younger brother was at home with his parents and that his brother "was really enjoying himself." It made Bill very angry to be mistreated and to know that his brother was getting so much while he was getting so little.

After Bill ventilated a lot of anger and cried a bit, he turned to the social worker and asked, "Are you going to the carnival tonight?" When Mr. H asked, "What makes you ask?" Bill responded, "Come with me, I'll show you how to toast hot dogs!" Mr. H consented warmly.

Like so many clients, Bill needed somebody to listen to him. When he was given the opportunity to ventilate anger, criticize the camp, voice his yearning to be loved, and express his sibling rivalry, his anxiety and distress diminished a great deal. It should be noted that the social worker said very little to Bill but was obviously very helpful to him. When Bill asked a question, the social worker appropriately tried to get to his client's motives for asking it rather than answer it. As a result, the client could show his real need—a need for human contact.

Many clinicians, particularly during the early interviews with their clients, believe that they should answer their clients' questions about the therapists' qualifications, theoretical biases, preferred treatment modalities, and the like. What is always important for the clinician to keep in mind, as we suggested earlier in this chapter, is that when clients ask questions of the practitioner, they are covering up feelings, thoughts, doubts, and conflicts. It is much better to respond to a client's question with "What are you feeling now, when you ask the question?" than it is to answer the question. Answers to questions by the therapist frequently squelch what clients are feeling and thinking. Feelings and thoughts of clients should be verbalized and understood, not suppressed.

Although good listening is a necessity in good interviewing, no interviewee wants a completely passive and silent listener. As the interviews progress, the therapist slowly involves himself or herself verbally. One of the central procedures in good interviewing is posing good questions. Questions are asked to elicit pertinent data in order to arrive at a comprehensive psychosocial assessment; they are also posed to help clients explore and reflect on their roles in interpersonal relationships, and they are frequently asked in order to ascertain how clients are feeling toward the therapist and about the therapy. A question that truly engages clients is one that clarifies ambiguities, completes a picture of their situations, elicits emotional responses, and helps them reflect more on their modus operandi (Kadushin, 1972).

In order for a question to be experienced by the client as helpful, he or she has to experience it as one that, if answered fully, will enhance him or her in some way. Questions that can be answered with "Yes" or "No" or "I don't know" do not really help clients discharge feelings and thoughts, explore their situations more fully, or increase their self-understanding. Asking a client, "Are you happy on your job?" gives the client limited opportunity to reflect on his or her job, discharge complaints, or examine his or her interactions on the job. However, if the practitioner asks, "Could you tell me how it is going on your job?" or "How do you get along on your job?" more data will be elicited and a fuller exploration of the client's job functioning may ensue.

Questions have to be phrased so that they can be understood. They should be short, simple, and unambiguous. Perhaps of more importance than the precise formulation of a question is the attitude with which it is presented. Clients should feel that the question evolves from the clinician's empathy and identification with them. This helps clients want to talk more freely and in more depth.

Empathic questions supplement good listening. The following brief examples illustrate this.

Fred and Joan Samuels, a couple in their thirties, were seen for a consultation to discuss their deteriorating marriage. During the course of their interview with Mr. G, the therapist, they hurled insults at each other, and each tried to demonstrate to Mr. G that the other was provoking a battle. When they saw that Mr. G was not going to be manipulated into siding with one against the other, they stopped fighting for a while. However, if Fred became more conciliatory, Joan would fight with him, and when Joan was softer, Fred initiated a battle. When this pattern became quite clear to Mr. G, he asked the Samuels, "What bothers each of you about being liked?" After a long silence, Joan pensively stated, "I guess it makes me uncomfortable. I don't know why. Yet, when Fred shows warmth, I cringe." Fred acknowledged that he, too, was uncomfortable with intimacy. The couple could now move into more productive sessions with Mr. G.

When Bob and Jean Tolstoy, a couple in their late thirties, came to the child guidance clinic to see if they could place their 10-year-old son, Harvey, in a home for delinquent children, they described Harvey in psychological terms without expressing any feelings toward him. They described Harvey's "defective superego," his "weak ego," and his "unconscious wish to destroy." After listening for about twenty minutes to the Tolstoys' attempts to mask their distress by intellectualizing, Ms. F, the social worker, asked, "How does it feel to live with a youngster who appears so out of control?" Within several seconds, Bob and Jean began to talk about how Harvey was "exasperating," "gets us furious," and "makes us feel helpless and hopeless."

After voicing their anger, despair, and hurt for the next twenty minutes, Bob, with Jean agreeing, said, "Maybe we should talk this over some more with Ms. F before we do something."

In addition to listening attentively and asking well-timed questions, the clinician also comments at appropriate times. He or she will *confront* the client with certain clear impressions, *clarify* the meaning of certain patterns, and *interpret* the meaning of certain behavior to the client. While treatment procedures will be discussed in more detail in Chapter 5, in the early interviews the practitioner has to make certain comments at times. In the initial stages of working with clients, most comments are made to help them face their fears of getting involved in treatment and/or their fears of revealing themselves. For example, to a silent, inarticulate client, the therapist might comment, "There seems to be something about me which makes you feel uncomfortable." To a belligerent, provocative client, "You are feeling very upset about being here" might be helpful. These are leading remarks designed to encourage clients to reflect on their attitudes and behavior.

To reiterate, many clinicians are too eager to clarify, advise, or interpret in order to feel that they are helpful people. Therapists often make comments to diminish their own anxiety rather than to assist their clients. While any comment of the clinician's can be rationalized, many of them are unnecessary. The good interviewer is a good listener and one who asks well-timed questions. When making comments, he or she is taking a stand and therefore should be very sure that the observation is correct and the client is ready to accept it. In the early interviews, continued listening with occasional questions is rarely destructive to clients, but bombarding them with comments can activate anxiety and increase defensiveness.

Like questions, comments should be brief and clear. Furthermore, the therapist's use of language should take into consideration the client's social, economic, and cultural circumstances. The sensitive practitioner recognizes language differences among different ethnic, socioeconomic, and age groups and flexibly adjusts his or her own choice of words so that clients can feel that the practitioner is in their particular life-space, empathically listening.

REFERENCES

Barbara, D. (1958). *The art of listening*. Springfield, IL: Charles C Thomas.

Blanck, G., & Blanck, R. (1974). *Ego psychology: Theory and practice*. New York: Columbia University Press.

Fine, R. (1982). *The healing of the mind* (2nd ed.). New York: Free Press.

Hamilton, G. (1951). *Theory and practice of social casework*. New York: Columbia University Press.

Kadushin, A. (1972). *The social work interview*. New York: Columbia University Press.

Langs, R. (1981). *Resistances and interventions*. New York: Jason Aronson.

Perlman, H. (1968). *Persona: Social role and personality*. Chicago: University of Chicago Press.

Schafer, R. (1983). *The analytic attitude*. New York: Basic Books.

Spotnitz, H. (1976). *Psychotherapy of preoedipal disorders*. New York: Jason Aronson.

Strean, H. (1985). *Resolving resistances in psychotherapy*. New York: John Wiley.

Strean, H. (1984). The patient who would not give his name. *Psychoanalytic Quarterly, 53*, 410-420.

Strean, H. (1978). *Clinical social work*. New York: Free Press.

Chapter 2

THE PSYCHOSOCIAL ASSESSMENT

In order to help an individual, a marital dyad, or a family, the therapist must *assess* what is troubling his or her clients and why it is troubling them. Making an assessment represents the thinking of the practitioner about the facts that have been gathered on the client or clients. The assessment "is a professional opinion that is influenced by the frame of reference that [the practitioner] uses to guide him in understanding the meaning of the facts" (Hollis, 1964, p. 251).

It was recognized very early in clinical work that an assessment is no better than the facts it rests on (Richmond, 1917). If a therapist has not gathered the necessary facts about the client's personality, interpersonal functioning, history, and current situation, the assessment will be superficial. A superficial assessment, of course, results in a superficial treatment plan, and the client will receive only limited help. However, if the clinician gathers substantial data, there is a good chance that a comprehensive psychosocial assessment will evolve; this strengthens the possibility of formulating an individualized treatment plan tailored to the client's ego strengths, conflicts, history, and current social circumstances. Mary Richmond, the founder of social casework, pointed out in *Social Diagnosis* (1917) that a practitioner, in order to gather facts, "must open his eyes and look; in [assessment] you close them and think."

How an assessment will emerge is, in many ways, going to be a function of the practitioner's view of personality functioning, his or her view of how people are affected by their past and present interpersonal and social circumstances, his or her view of what is maladaptive, and his or her aims and goals for the client (Langs, 1981). A Jungian therapist may view a client's fear of asserting himself as "a clash between collective and individual loyalties" (G. Adler, 1967), whereas a Freudian therapist may view the same problem as emanating from the client's unresolved Oedipal conflict (Fenichel, 1945).

In this chapter and in succeeding ones, we will refer to a "psychosocial" assessment because we take the position that people and their social situations are always in dynamic interaction and that both contribute to adaptation and maladaptation. For example, if a child is suffering from a school phobia, the therapist in assessing the youngster's separation anxiety will want to understand how the child's internal wishes, fears, and prohibitions interact and transact with his parents', teachers', and neighborhood's mandates, wishes, and reinforcements. To understand the child's psychological functioning, he cannot be viewed as separate from his social context or vice versa.

The therapist with a psychosocial orientation asserts that behavior cannot be assessed accurately until a full study of the person-situation constellation is made. A school phobia for a child in a deteriorated slum may have much different meaning than it has for a child in an affluent neighborhood. An anxiety about being raped will probably have a much different meaning for one walking in New York City at night than it does for a person roaming the countryside in the morning.

Professional judgments have to be supported by evidence and reason; they have to be checked and rechecked. As we have already implied, they take into consideration the client's current behavior in and out of his therapy, his or her psychodynamics, situation, and modes of relating to the therapist and to others. The clinician does not rush to any conclusion but makes sure that the assessment meets logical and professional criteria—that is, the assessment derives from facts that should be apparent to another professional. In sum, the assessment should be one that is valid, and reliable (Strean, 1978; Hamilton, 1951; Hollis, 1972).

In this chapter, we will present and discuss the necessary components of a verifiable psychosocial assessment. In addition to discussing an assessment on individual clients, we will also briefly look at some of the features of a psychosocial assessment on marital dyads and on families. We will conclude our discussion with a brief consideration of clinical categories: the neuroses, psychoses, character disorders, and so on.

ASSESSING THE CLIENT'S PERSONALITY

Many researchers of personality have taken the position that the most meticulous and comprehensive presentation of a theory of personality is that of Sigmund Freud (Hall & Lindzey, 1957; Fine, 1979;

Hollis, 1972; Hamilton, 1958). While there are many practitioners and theorists in social work and in other helping professions who would disagree with this statement (Fischer, 1976; Briar & Miller, 1971; Borenzweig, 1971; Mahoney & Mahoney, 1974), for purposes of having a comprehensive assessment of the person in therapy, we believe that the Freudian psychoanalytic position has much to offer.

In contrast to many other theories of personality, which explain only fragments of the human being, Freud postulated the principle of *psychic determinism*. This principle holds that in mental functioning nothing happens by chance. Everything that a person feels, thinks, does, fantasizes, and dreams has psychological motives. Whom the client chooses to marry, how he or she makes a living, where the person lives, who are the person's friends—are all motivated by *unconscious* inner forces (S. Freud, 1939).

Although situational factors are always impinging on the client, the client interprets them and copes with them in his or her unique, idiosyncratic ways. The notion of psychic determinism and the unconscious help the clinician to recognize not only that the behavior of individuals, dyads, and families is a direct reaction to external variables such as family, job, and neighborhood, but also that how clients experience these variables is shaped by unique wishes, defenses, anxieties, ethical imperatives, hopes, fears, and history.

> When Sam Abrams, age 36, discussed in a therapy group that he had been married three times, exploration of his relationships revealed that all three of his wives were experienced by him as "dominating," "castrating," and "belligerent." As Sam's interaction with group members was examined and as his own history unfolded, it turned out that Sam had a strong, unconscious wish to be punished by a mother figure whom he hated. As Sam concluded, "It's more than a coincidence that I find myself constantly ending up with angry dames."

Freud (1938, 1939) saw the human personality from five distinct but intermeshing points of view: the structural, the genetic, the topographic, the dynamic, and the economic. Let us look at each of these five approaches and consider how their use can help us with the making of a comprehensive psychosocial assessment.

THE STRUCTURAL APPROACH

The structural approach refers to the psychic structure of id, ego, and superego. The id, the most primitive part of the mind and totally unconscious, is the repository of sexual and aggressive drives and is concerned with their gratification. The ego, which develops largely out of experience and reason, is the executive part of the personality and mediates between the inner world of id wishes, superego commands, and the demands of the external world. Some of the functions of the ego are judgment, reality testing, impulse control, frustration tolerance, and relating to other people; the ego also erects defenses against anxiety. The superego is the judge or censor of the mind and is essentially the product of interpersonal experiences. It is the storehouse of "do's and don'ts" (the conscience) as well as the container of values and ethical imperatives (the ego-ideal).

The id, ego, and superego are always in dynamic interaction. By understanding this interaction in the client, the therapist can secure valuable information for the assessment. The practitioner has to determine which id wishes are being opposed by the superego and/or the external environment and also how the client's ego copes with this struggle. Does the client's ego submit to the superego and renounce the id wish? Does the client's ego gratify the id wish and then later arrange for punishment? Or does the client enlist his or her ego functions to rebel against superego mandates?

The following examples demonstrate how clients' problems can be assessed, in part, by observing the interaction of id wishes, ego functions, and superego mandates:

> When the therapist tried to assess 30-year-old Bill Barker's inability to be sexually potent with his wife, the therapist was able to determine that Bill had strong, hostile fantasies toward his wife (id expression) which his superego opposed. Every time Bill was sexually stimulated, he felt very anxious because the reasoning part of his ego distorted sex and he concluded that by having sex, he was discharging forbidden hostile desires. Bill's ego submitted to his superego, and he unconsciously arranged for his penis to be flaccid.

> Treatment helped Bill to weaken the power of his punitive superego. This enabled the reasoning and judgment parts of his ego to become more tolerant of his id wishes. With his ego more accepting of his id desires, his potency was restored.

> Joyce Carter, a single woman in her mid-twenties, sought therapeutic help because she found herself rejecting men as soon as she started to feel close to them. Her therapist was able to determine that whenever Joyce became emotionally and sexually intimate with a man, she unconsciously made him a father figure (id wish). Closeness with a man, therefore, activated

incestuous wishes toward her partner which her superego opposed. Her superego punished her ego for entertaining incestuous wishes; by rejecting men (ego operation), Joyce could placate her superego, reduce her guilt, and renounce those id wishes of hers which created anxiety.

As Joyce could discuss her incestuous desires with her therapist (a benign superego), she began to feel less guilty about her id wishes and her ego did not have to participate in rejecting men as much.

Jordan David, a 10-year-old boy, was seen in a child guidance clinic because, despite his high IQ, he could not read. In studying his client, the therapist discovered that Jordan was a boy who was strongly pushed by his parents to constantly achieve. Internalizing his parents' harsh admonitions, Jordan developed a very punitive and harsh superego and could not like himself unless he was close to perfect.

Jordan's inability to read was an expression of his ego constantly rebelling against his superego's commands. By raging at his introjected parental voices that he would not comply with their mandates, many of his ego functions were joining with his hostile id wishes against his superego. His refusal to read was his ego's protest against his superego.

When Jordan, in his play-therapy, could be supported and encouraged by his therapist as he aggressed toward parental figures and was reinforced when he decided "not to work so hard," he began to read.

Ellen Emmer, a 22-year-old single woman, sought therapeutic help because she suffered from intermittent bouts of depression and frequent psychosomatic problems: migraine headaches, insomnia, asthma, and backaches. After working with her for several months, her therapist was able to conclude that her intermittent depressions and frequent somatic difficulties were unconscious punishments by her superego for her attempts to achieve successfully. Ellen was a very competitive young woman whose ego, everytime she allowed herself pleasure for succeeding (id gratification), felt compelled to accept superego punishment a couple of days later. To Ellen, success meant that she had vanquished her enemies; consequently, her ego had to accept superego punishment which took the form of depression and bodily aches and pains.

When Ellen could see that fantasies of killing her competitors were a lot different from actually murdering them, she could begin to accept her successful achievements with more equanimity.

Ego psychologists (A. Freud, 1937; Erikson, 1950; Hartmann, 1951) conceptualized the ego as something more than Freud's "mediator." They began to see it as a structure with autonomy and power of its own.

The ego's power arises primarily from the development of "the secondary process"—those aspects of the ego that are rational, adapted to reality, and derive from interpersonal processes and experiences: locomotion, cognition, memory, perception, and rational thought and action.

By applying aspects of ego psychology to practice, the clinician can assess the level of the client's perceptive, executive, and integrative functions: "Have the ego's defenses been overdeveloped?" "Is the client's social situation such that his defenses are vitally necessary adaptations to it, as in the environment of a downtrodden ghetto?'

One of the most important ego functions to which all helping professionals must give attention is that of the client's defenses—those ego mechanisms which protect the client from anxiety. The defenses include *projection* (ascribing to others one's own unacceptable feelings, thoughts, or behaviors, as does the client who finds his sexual and aggressive fantasies abhorrent and tells the therapist that every time he comes into the therapist's office, he knows that the therapist himself is full of hostile and erotic thoughts); *denial* (averring that something that appears anxiety-provoking, such as an illness, the loss of a job, or the imminent death of a loved one, simply does not exist); and *isolation* (separating emotions from thoughts because, experienced together, they appear overwhelming, as does the client who has intense hostile feelings and thoughts but finds that his mind is "blank," although he feels strong heart palpitations, or the client who feels nothing but is obsessed with murderous thoughts). Other defenses used by the ego are turning against the self, regression, undoing, repression, and reaction formation.

On the client's feeling certain emotions toward another person but finding them unacceptable, he or she can *turn against the self*. For example, upon feeling angry toward his therapist but worried that the therapist would dislike him for it, Mr. Frank would say, "You are such a nice person, how can I be angry at you? I'm really a horrible person who should be scorned by you!" In this defense, the individual prefers to attack himself rather than attack the person at whom he is angry.

If reality presents a danger, the client *regresses* by returning to an immature form of functioning that is more gratifying than his current situation. A child who has achieved toilet training may regress to soiling and bedwetting when the demands of school or home appear too much to bear.

Undoing is a defense that has as its aim to eradicate the harm which the client thinks may be caused by his aggressive or sexual fantasies. A client who feels very guilty about sadistic fantasies may become a compulsive rescuer and "do-gooder" to placate his or her punitive superego.

Repression bars from consciousness id impulses that cause anxiety. Like all defensive activity, this process is always unconscious. No client is ever consciously aware that he or she is repressing, undoing, and the like.

Reaction formation is a defense mechanism whereby one of a pair of ambivalent attitudes is rendered unconscious by overemphasizing the other. For example, almost every time Ms. Gold experienced erotic fantasies toward her male therapist, she would say "You are so ugly and so stupid. I hate you."

In the use of all defense mechanisms, there is frequently an attempt to repudiate an impulse (A. Freud, 1937). In response to the id's "yes," the ego defends by saying "no" to avoid the danger of a forbidden impulse becoming conscious. However, the ego can also defend against the voices of the superego. Many clients try to deny and project guilt rather than face it. For example, many clients will say to their therapists, "I never felt guilt until I met you. You *make* me feel guilty."

Seemingly irrational, provocative behavior that appears upsetting to the practitioner can often be understood and related to empathically if the practitioner is aware that all human beings defend themselves from ideas and feelings that arouse anxiety.

Mr. Z, a social worker in a mental health center, was becoming increasingly upset with his client Bob Hill, a married man of 27 years. The upset did not subside until Mr. Z began to think of Bob's defense mechanisms and what kind of anxiety they attempted to ward off.

Bob would come into interviews with Mr. Z and tell him that his life was great. The only thing that bothered Bob was his very "stupid" wife, who was "completely incompetent." Bob realized that he would "just have to accept" his "stupid wife" because Mr. Z looked like "a depressed fairy" who could not help him very much. Maybe, Bob mused, he could help Mr. Z.

As Mr. Z studied his irritation with Bob, he realized that because Bob felt so vulnerable and had such a low self-esteem, he had to *deny* his problems. Furthermore, Bob felt so inept about his capacity to cope that he *projected* his feelings. Apparently the helping situation aroused warm feelings in Bob. He *repressed* these feelings and coped with the intolerable anxiety that his homosexual fantasies induced by projecting them onto Mr. Z and calling him "a fairy."

THE GENETIC APPROACH

Each individual's past participates in and shapes his present. Most people, for example, select spouses who remind them, to some extent, of the parents of their past. Arguments and conflicts between friends and colleagues are frequently a recapitulation of past sibling battles. Parents also tend to relive their relationships with their own parents with their children.

During the first five or six years of life, the child experiences a series of differentiated dynamic stages that are of enormous importance in the formation of personality. In the oral stage, the mouth is the principal focus of activity; in the anal phase, the child turns his interests to eliminative functions; in the phallic stage, he or she forms the rudiments of a sexual identity; in latency, there is a quiescence of erotic interest; and at puberty, there is a recrudescence of biological drives, particularly of the Oedipal interests that emerged during the phallic phase, and ambivalence toward parents and other figures of authority (S. Freud, 1939).

Erik Erikson (1950) expanded Freud's genetic approach by placing psychosexual development within a social matrix and by emphasizing the tasks of ego mastery presented by each stage of maturation. He identified eight conflicts in the life span: trust versus mistrust, autonomy versus shame and doubt, initiative versus guilt, industry versus inferiority, identity versus role diffusion, intimacy versus isolation, generativity versus stagnation, and integrity versus despair. These conflicts correspond to Freud's stages of orality, anality, phallic-Oedipal, latency, puberty, and so forth.

One of the key contributions of Erikson is his postulation that human functioning cannot be viewed apart from the social context in which it transpires. For example, the infant's functioning during the oral phase cannot be assessed without taking into consideration the infant's transactions with the mother. If the infant and mother mutually gratify each other, the child will learn to "trust" rather than "distrust" others. Similarly, if the youngster is helped to forgo certain infantile pleasures and learns to cope with frustration during toilet training (anal phase), he or she will develop a sense of "autonomy" rather than experience doubt and shame.

Two important notions inherent in the genetic approach are *regression* and *fixation*. Regression, as we have already said, is the client's attempt to go back to a time of more immature functioning because the present is too anxiety-provoking. Fixation refers to that operation by which the client stays at an early development level in much of his or her functioning, because to move on is too frightening. The reason that these two notions are so important in assessment is that the same symptom can be a regression for one person and a fixation for another. Unless the therapist knows which is taking place, treatment is haphazard.

> Jerry Isaac, age 27, was a chronic alcoholic. His mother was a very depressed woman who divorced his father before Jerry's birth. Jerry had not received any warmth or tenderness from any mother figure and harbored a great deal of anger and distrust toward virtually everyone. He had never loved anyone, and his major gratification was "my bottle." Jerry reflected about his bottle, "It's always there and tastes good." Jerry was *fixated* at the oral level and was full of distrust. In his treatment he needed to spend considerable time voicing his anger and getting in touch with infantile yearnings before he could mature.

> Burt Joseph, age 28, also sought help with his problem of alcoholism. As a child, Burt had a very seductive relationship with his mother who often bathed with him and cuddled him in bed. This went on well into puberty.

> When Burt married, he began to dread being close to his wife. Although he had all kinds of rationalizations to account for his disinterest in sex and intimacy, Burt clearly had unconsciously made his wife a mother figure and was frightened of experiencing incestuous fantasies when with her. To cope with his anxiety about being close to his wife, he "went out with the boys." When the closeness with men bothered him, to dissipate his anxiety, he drank. Burt *regressed* from the position of being an Oedipal boy (sex with his wife was experienced as sex with mother) to a latent homosexual position—"going out with the boys." When being with the boys aroused anxiety, he *regressed* again, to an oral position—drinking alcohol.

> In his treatment, Burt needed to focus on his wishes to make his wife a mother, and he also needed to reduce his guilt for these wishes. On doing so, his alcoholism diminished greatly.

As part of the assessment, the practitioner has to determine how the client is misperceiving others—spouse, children, employer, colleagues, friends, and the therapist—as if they were people in the client's past. Furthermore, the therapist has to determine where the client is in terms of his or her psychosocial growth. Has he or she ever learned to trust?

Has the client established sufficient ego autonomy? Or, what is inducing stress in the client that is causing a regression? These questions have to be answered correctly before the clinician can form a helpful treatment plan.

THE TOPOGRAPHIC APPROACH

The topographical approach refers to the conscious, preconscious, and unconscious states of mind. The conscious is that part of our mental activities of which we are fully aware at any time; the preconscious refers to thoughts and feelings that can be summoned into consciousness quite easily; the unconscious refers to feelings, thoughts, and desires of which we are *not* aware but which constantly influence our thinking, feeling, and behavior. The unconscious consists of wishes, defenses, and superego mandates as well as memories of events and attitudes that have been repressed (S. Freud, 1938, 1939). It is only when unconscious wishes emerge in dreams, fantasies, slips of the tongue, or neurotic and psychotic symptoms that the unconscious becomes known. Otherwise, it acts silently and beyond the awareness of the person.

One of the main characteristics of the unconscious is the *primary process*, a type of mental functioning that is nonrational. It is best observed in dreams, which are frequently illogical or primitive and do not adhere to the laws of reality. For example, in a dream, an ambitious wish might be symbolized by flying an airplane by oneself. Contrasted to the primary process is the *secondary process*, which governs conscious thinking. It is logical, rational, and obeys the laws of reality.

One of the basic tenets of Freudian psychoanalysis is that the unconscious is always operative in all behavior, adaptive and maladaptive. This perspective leads the clinician who is making an assessment to ask why the client who consistently fails in love relationships *unconsciously* wants to fail, or why the client who does not succeed on the job unconsciously wants it that way. It helps the practitioner recognize that every chronic marital complaint of a spouse about the partner is an unconscious wish; for example, the man who constantly says his wife is cold and rejecting unconsciously wants such a wife (Strean, 1985).

If a marital pair constantly avoid each other emotionally and sexually, the therapist looks to see what he or she can learn about why this arrangement unconsciously protects them.

Paul and Bertha Hammer, a young couple in their mid-twenties, sought marriage counseling because they both felt very alienated from each other. Their emotional withdrawal was very apparent in their counseling sessions but was intensified when warmth was expressed by one to the other or toward Ms. W, the counselor. When this issue became the focus of treatment, Paul and Bertha were able to discover that their withdrawal was unconsciously needed because warmth conjured up, for both of them, feelings of being a dependent child, and they wanted "to avoid feeling childish and needy."

When they could talk about their childish and dependent wishes with Ms. W and with each other, Paul and Bertha did not need their defense of withdrawal as much and could relate to each other with more spontaneity.

The topographic point of view states that to understand and help a client, the unconscious meaning of the client's behavior should be well understood. Because unconscious wishes, defenses, mandates, and memories strongly influence self-image, self-esteem, and all interpersonal behavior, the unconscious is an indispensable concept in assessment and treatment.

THE DYNAMIC APPROACH

The dynamic point of view refers to Freud's instinct theory, which is concerned with the libidinal drives. An instinct, according to Freud, has four characteristics: a source, an aim, an object, and an impetus. The source is a bodily condition, that is, a need, such as hunger, sex, or aggression. The aim is to release tension and to receive gratification. The object includes both the object on which the drive is focused, such as food, and all the activities necessary to secure it. The impetus of an instinct is its strength, which is determined by the force or intensity of the underlying need. A need varies in quantity in different individuals or in the same individual at different times.

In making an assessment, the therapist wants to ascertain if the client's instincts are being gratified. Is the client getting enough food and enjoying it? If not, why not? Is the client realistically being deprived and/or is he unconsciously arranging to be deprived? Does gratifying the hunger instinct create anxiety for the client, and is that why he or she does not want to eat too much? Similar questions may be asked of the client regarding his or her elimination habits and his or her sex life. The answers to these questions help the therapist pinpoint conflict, plan intervention, gauge the client's motivation, and determine his or her capacity to participate in a therapeutic relationship.

Abraham Joseph, a 10-year-old boy, was seen in a child guidance clinic by Mr. V. Early in his contact with Abraham, Mr. V noted that his client was very much underweight, was very depressed, and could not concentrate in school, or elsewhere.

Investigation of Abraham's life revealed that his symptoms were exacerbated a few weeks after he was placed in a foster home. While the foster home was a warm setting, in which his foster parents gave him a great deal—food, clothing, recreation, and emotional responsiveness—Abraham became more and more depressed.

In his play therapy with Mr. V, Abraham was able to reveal that he was rejecting food and other gratifications because he felt very guilty. His guilt was due to the fact that he felt he had a much better deal than any of his three siblings. Feeling that he was "a mean brother," he deprived himself of instinctual gratification to appease his guilt. When Mr. V helped him understand that he was not really depriving his siblings, he did not have to deprive himself of instinctual gratification as much as he had been doing.

THE ECONOMIC APPROACH

The economic point of view stresses the quantitative factor in mental functioning. According to this principle, all behavior is regulated by the need to dispose of psychological energy. Energy is discharged by forming *cathexes*; that is, something (or somebody) is *cathected* if it is emotionally significant to the client.

Freud believed that energy is needed to fuel the psychic structure, and he saw this energy coming from the sexual drive. Later, Hartmann (1964) concluded that the ego works with "deaggressivized" and "desexualized" energy, which he called "neutral" energy. The energy concept is among that most controversial in the field, and many theoreticians contend that it can be dispensed with entirely (Fine, 1973).

ASSESSING THE CLIENT'S SITUATION

As we have implied several times in this chapter, no client is an island standing completely alone. He or she is always being affected by interactions and transactions with other people. Regardless of the client's unique psychodynamics, the client's "significant others" may enhance his or her functioning, hurt it, or keep it in relative equilibrium (Bertalanffy, 1968); therefore, relationships with "significant others" must always be assessed. In clinical work, the client's *situation* refers to his or her relationships with significant others. The client's situation defines his or her role, status, identity, and responsibilities in various social contexts: at home, at school, with extended family, in the neighborhood, and so on.

When clinicians assess the situational components in their clients' life-spaces, they frequently come to appreciate how their "significant others" are contributing to their psychological problems. Consider, for example, a client on public welfare:

> The modal welfare client is an individual trapped in a vicious cycle of grinding poverty. . . . He is frequently living in a run-down neighborhood and exploited by landlords. Schools and other services in his locale are usually inferior; when physicians or attorneys are needed, his usual experience is to wait in long lines, and often he receives superficial help. The bulk of welfare clients are blind, disabled, or mothers of young children who must cope without husbands who have been shunned by the job market. . . . All too often the individual who ends up on welfare does so involuntarily, and this parallels the fact that he was frequently an involuntary victim of a broken home. Most frequently he has experienced limited emotional, physical, or economic satisfaction during his life. (Strean, 1978, p. 83)

THE CLIENT'S SITUATION AND THE DEFINITION OF THE PROBLEM

In many ways, an individual's social context defines whether he or she will or will not be a client. For example, if a homosexual man or homosexual woman lives in Greenwich Village in New York, his or her homosexuality will probably not be considered "a problem" by most of his or her "significant others" in Greenwich Village. However, if the same man or woman were to become a member of the U.S. Army and his or her sexual orientation was discovered by significant others, the individual would, in all likelihood, be quickly referred for psycho-therapy. If, on becoming a client, the individual did not want to renounce the homosexuality, he or she might be considered a candidate for a psychiatric discharge from the military.

Among certain ethnic groups, it is quite acceptable for husbands and wives to cope with their marital conflicts by physically striking each other from time to time. However, among other ethnic groups, identical behavior would be considered very inappropriate, perhaps very anti-social, and if the couple's physical assaults became known to significant others, the couple would be implored to seek therapeutic help.

Because social groups such as family, extended family, neighbors, and religious groups all have their own codes for acceptable and unacceptable behavior, individuals who compose these groups tend to judge themselves in accordance with them. A white, Anglo-Saxon Protestant Republican man might view his temporary unemployment with a great deal of alarm and feel that he needs therapeutic help immediately. However, a black man living in Harlem might respond to his temporary unemployment with less terror and might not feel in such dire need of treatment.

Whether an individual deems a certain type of behavior, such as homosexuality, extramarital activity, unemployment, or physical assault, a psychosocial problem depends in many ways on how his significant others define such behavior. Frequently an individual becomes a client when he or she is not living in accordance with the expectations set by significant others. He or she may feel guilty about opposing sanctions, feel angry about complying with them, or feel mixed emotions and tormented about what to do.

THE CLIENT'S SITUATION AND ACCEPTANCE OF THE CLIENT ROLE

Among many groups it is quite fashionable to be a client, while among others it is reprehensible. In working with a client, it is extremely important for the practitioner to ascertain whether the client's family, friends, and others support or negate the idea of therapy. All clients are influenced by what they perceive to be the attitudes of significant others toward psychotherapy. As with other social sanctions from others, some clients enjoy rebelling against their significant others' mandates, others like to cooperate, and many others are quite ambivalent.

When clients echo the attitudes of significant others toward treatment, even if they consciously disagree with these attitudes, they are always affected by them.

Sandra Katz, age 30, was in treatment for marital difficulties. Although she was gaining from her treatment, and although her husband was pleased with her progress, after her sixth session of treatment she began to arrive late for her appointments. When Ms. U, her therapist, explored her lateness with her, it turned out that Sandra's mother was against her therapy. Sandra, though consciously disagreeing with her mother's attitudes toward treatment, was affected by the latter's point of view. Unconsciously, Sandra viewed therapy as hurting her mother, and this issue had to be faced in her work with Ms. U.

Clients frequently remark that their relatives and friends are feeling threatened by their going into treatment. These significant others often do feel defensive about their own mental status when clients talk about their personal emotional problems. On many occasions, relatives and friends feel competitive with the therapist and/or fear that they will be rejected by the client. Clients often worry about these issues as well, and can believe that their treatment will force them to abandon significant others. These issues should be part of every assessment and treatment plan.

THE CLIENT AS A ROLE CARRIER
IN VARIOUS SOCIAL SYSTEMS

A social system is a group of individual actors in transaction who have interrelated tasks and the capacity for certain kinds of performance (Bertalanffy, 1968; Buckley, 1967; Compton & Galaway, 1975). Each actor in a social system influences the others. Consequently, one may consider a marital dyad, a parent-child relationship, or a family as a social system because each consists of transacting actors with interrelated tasks and interdependent functions.

For purposes of assessment, there are a few principles of social system theory which appear pertinent. According to the principle of *stability*, social systems theory emphasizes input and output, and the equilibriating processes that keep the system in a state of stability. Stability means that a change in one part of the system induces a change in the other parts. For example, if a mother starts going to work or a child leaves home or the parents separate, the behavior of the other members of the family will be modified in order to adapt to the change.

The principle of stability is a crucial one in assessing the client's interpersonal relationships. Often an individual becomes a client because he or she is reacting to a change in one of the systems in which he or she is a participant.

Calvin Lyman, age 40, sought help for a depression. Although he had bitterly complained about his wife Sheila's lack of interest in sex, he became upset with her when Sheila, after several months of therapy, began to become interested in sex. Mr. T, Calvin's therapist, in assessing the Lymans' marriage, was able to recognize that the couple were able to maintain a degree of stability as long as Sheila was disinterested in sex and Calvin could complain about it. When Sheila became interested in a more intimate relationship with Calvin, the stability of their marital subsystem was disrupted.

In a study conducted several years ago (Strean, 1970), an attempt was made to enlarge on the diagnostic assessment of Freud's six-year-old patient, Little Hans, who suffered from a phobia of horses. The study was able to demonstrate not only that Hans's phobia was a symptom expressing his unconscious sexual fantasies toward his mother and his hostile, competitive feelings toward his father, but also that marital, parent-child, and parent-parent subsystems all had to be assessed carefully in order to comprehend the full meaning of Hans's problems. In reexamining the data, it became quite clear that Hans's phobia also expressed his ambivalent feelings concerning his parents' tempestuous marriage. Inasmuch as Hans's phobia was one of the few concerns that Hans's parents shared, on Hans being cured of his phobia, the parents divorced.

A second principle of systems theory states that a system is *transactional*. A reciprocal relationship exists between all parts of the system. When an organism is "in process" with the environment, knowledge of the organism or environment alone is inadequate. The full system must be observed because important transactions occur between whatever people under discussion are involved with each other. By infusing psychosocial assessments with transactional processes, we can appreciate not only how one member affects another but also how their conjoint behavior is always influencing each of them. Not only are the partners in a marital subsystem constantly influencing each other, but the marital subsystem (husband and wife), parent-child subsystems, parent-parent subsystem (husband and wife in their roles as parents), and sibling subsystems are all influencing each other (Stein, 1971).

To recognize the profound implications and impact of transactional processes for purposes of a comprehensive psychosocial assessment, let us look at a case situation in which a child was ill with rheumatic fever.

When Shirley Macdonald, age 8, became ill, her mother panicked and became quite depressed. Mr. Macdonald resented his wife's withdrawal and reacted by becoming very critical of her. As a result, Mrs. Macdonald could not fully concentrate on helping Shirley recover and the doctor admonished both Mr. and Mrs. Macdonald for not attending to Shirley more fully.

Later, Mr. Macdonald's mother became infuriated with him for not visiting her more often. He, in turn, felt upset by his mother's criticism, and this induced him to blame Shirley for his mother's resentment toward him. He withdrew in anger, but lost sleep. His insomnia caused him to be late for work on several occasions, and he had to forfeit some of his salary; as a result, he could not pay the doctor on time. When the doctor threatened to abandon the case because he was angry about not being paid, Mr. Macdonald became even more depressed.

From the above example, we see that when two subsystems are in transaction because they have a common member, occurrences in one subsystem will affect the other. This is referred to as *input* from one subsystem to another. Mr. Macdonald's input at work induced tension between him and his boss. When Mr. Macdonald's mother became irritated with him, this fed back into several subsystems of the Macdonald family. *Feedback* from other systems intensified the tension in the Macdonald family and caused all family members to modify their behavior.

A third important feature of a social system is the *communication of information*. Communication is an essential feature of the transaction, and the manner in which it is related influences the reciprocity or lack of reciprocity between the members of the system. If feelings and thoughts are directly communicated without fear of retaliation, the system tends to move toward *stability*. However, if communication is indirect or suppressed, resentment arises between the members and the system can deteriorate (Ruesch, 1961; Spiegel, 1960).

Communication can be verbal or nonverbal. The presenter may convey a latent message in his or her overt statement, as in a *double-bind* message (for example, the mother who admonishes her child, "Be careful as you go downstairs that you don't fall, smash your teeth, break your arms, and bleed to death!"). In the double-bind message, the speaker overtly manifests one set of intentions that only superficially mask other intentions, usually hostile ones, but often there can be muffled sexual ones as well. In assessing dyads and families, and individuals as well, a look at their communication patterns can be quite revealing.

In studying the communication patterns of the Notkin family, Ms. S, the family therapist, noted that whenever the parents were angry at the children or vice versa, they would concomitantly hug one another. As this pattern was studied, it became clear that all family members were very frightened of their intense angry feelings toward one another and that the hugging was a way of diluting them.

An aspect of a social system that is often overlooked is the *hierarchical factor*, with its implications for communication patterns and relationships among the system's members. A social structure that emphasizes status differences often creates barriers in communication (Stanton & Schwartz, 1954). When assessing clients in prisons, hospitals, schools, and the military, the hierarchical factor is very pertinent.

In assessing the ego functioning of several patients in a mental hospital, the social worker, Mr. R, was able to demonstrate that when the patients were no longer obliged to wear uniforms, were addressed by name rather than by number, and were offered statuses in the "Citizens' Council" of the mental hospital, their behavior changed remarkably. When the hospital system, in effect, ascribed a different status to the patients and began to view them as active participants in the hospital, their self-esteem, impulse control, and other ego functions improved dramatically.

The social context in which behavior is enacted always affects the practitioner's assessment. If mental patients are treated as second-class citizens, they will, of course, be assessed that way. If depressed and tormented clients are given statuses of "hard to reach" and "poorly motivated," they will be assessed accordingly.

In the various social systems in which clients participate, they enact different roles. When viewing clients as role carriers, one may be able to assess them more objectively. For example, Mr. Jones may not be simply a victim of a sadistic wife; he may receive some satisfaction and protection in enacting a masochistic role, or he might have left the marriage a long time ago. This same perspective can be utilized in assessing employer-employee relationships, parent-child interactions, and a host of other interpersonal relationships.

Stability, equilibrium, and integration of a social system are achieved through the *complementarity* of roles. Complementarity exists when a role partner carries out the reciprocal role automatically and without difficulty. In the assessment of marital relationships, the notion of complementarity is particularly useful.

When Ms. P, the marriage counselor, interviewed Mrs. Olsen to try to understand some of the etiological factors of her alcoholism, her initial assessment was based exclusively on Mrs. Olsen's psychodynamics and personal history. Later interviews with Mr. Olsen enlarged Ms. P's understanding. It became quite clear that although Mr. Olsen overtly repudiated his wife's drinking, he was vicariously enjoying it. This was evidenced by his going for walks with her to bars and giving her bottles of whiskey as presents. As a willing accomplice to his wife's drinking, Mr. Olsen could be regarded as her complementary role partner in alcoholism.

As part of the assessment, the client's role conflicts should be included. *Role conflict* occurs when the status of a member is defined differently by two reference groups (Rosenblatt, 1961). For example, many wives are in conflict between feeling pressed to enact a nurturing role at home and a managerial role at work. When they become clients, this role conflict can be expressed as follows: "I have so many demands on me. My husband and kids want me at home for dinner, but my boss wants me at the company dance. I'm torn and don't know which way to turn." Students are often tormented by a role conflict in which they feel an obligation to get good grades and study hard, but in doing so worry that they may be rejected by their peer groups.

ASSESSING THE MARITAL PAIR

Whether a client is being seen individually or with the spouse, his or her marital interactions should be carefully assessed. Clinicians have observed that only two happy and mature individuals can have a happy and mature marriage. Marriage never made an unhappy individual happy, nor did it turn a happy individual into an unhappy one (Strean, 1985).

Marriage counselors, as we have already implied, have learned that in every marriage there is a complementarity of roles. For every sadist there is a masochist; for every celibate, there is a partner who is reinforcing the sexual abstinence; and for every deceiver there is a role partner who wants, albeit unconsciously, to be deceived. Furthermore, practitioners who have treated people for their marital problems have been able to conclude that beneath every chronic marital complaint is an unconscious wish. The husband who habitually complains that his wife is cold and frigid needs and wants such a wife—a warm, receptive one would upset him. A wife who forever complains that her husband is passive and weak needs and wants such a husband—a strong and assertive man would upset her.

In assessing an individual or couple's marital problems, the practitioner should listen very carefully to the marital complaints. By doing so, the practitioner can eventually help the client or clients to see how they are arranging for the very marital problems they consciously declare they do not want to have.

> Rena Potter, age 32, constantly complained that her husband, Jay, was "terribly unromantic." He never brought flowers home, hardly every brought her perfume, and was extremely inept sexually. One day, Jay, instead of complaining that Rena was "a ball buster," made a determined effort to try to please her and brought home some flowers and some expensive perfume. At first Rena seem pleased, but when Jay and Rena were having sex later in the evening, Rena turned to Jay and asked impatiently, "How come your penis is so small?" Jay reacted by becoming impotent and for weeks withdrew from Rena sexually and emotionally, and stopped trying to be attentive to her. Rena could now, with some justification, declare that Jay was an inattentive husband and lover.

As is quite clear from the above case illustration, there is frequent unconscious collusion between marital partners in that they cooperate to sustain and reinforce their individual conflicts. Rena Potter needed and wanted an unassertive husband, and Jay cooperated by fulfilling this role. Jay, in turn, needed and wanted a woman who would demean him, and Rena cooperated with him in this venture. When Jay departed from his habitual way of coping in the marriage and became more assertive and more sexual, Rena was threatened by it and attempted to demean Jay. Once again, Jay colluded with Rena and became the passive man she wanted, while Rena resumed the role of the critical wife that Jay unconsciously desired.

When the notion of collusion (Eisenstein, 1956) is utilized by the practitioner in assessing clients' marital problems, there are really no saints and no sinners, and there are no innocent victims and no guilty abusers. Rather, both partners are seen as unconsciously at work protecting themselves from anxiety. In an implicit manner, both partners form a contract to preserve each other's neurosis by perceiving the partner as the partner needs to perceive himself or herself. Spouses unconsciously make their partners punitive superegos, forbidden ids, devaluated self-images, perfect ego-ideals, and so on. These issues must be part of every comprehensive psychosocial assessment.

ASSESSING THE FAMILY

As we stated earlier in this chapter, the family is a social system in which each member affects the others. In assessing an individual or a family, the practitioner should understand how and why each family member affects the others. The notion of "family homeostasis" (Jackson, 1957) provides a framework for the study of those conscious and unconscious forces that help to keep the family in equilibrium and those "inputs" that disturb the equilibrium. For example, a married couple may be able to interact harmoniously until the birth of a child. In helping the couple reach a new homeostatic balance that includes their child, the practitioner will assess not only how each of the marital partners emotionally experiences the baby; in addition, the practitioner will want to assess how the couple now experience each other as parents and how the advent of the baby influences the perception of each other as sexual partners (Zilbach, 1968).

Earlier we referred to the principle of *communication* in social systems. Communication has to be assessed in terms of the family members' unconscious wishes, fantasies, and defenses. The double-bind messages in which clients participate help us assess dysfunctional behavior. Many a disobedient child is fulfilling the unconscious message of his or her parents to disobey, and many an overcompliant youngster is unconsciously obeying the latent messages of his or her parents' communications.

As is true in marital interaction where each spouse's perception of the other can be distorted because of unrealistic wishes and fears originating from his or her relationship with his (her) parents, likewise parents can experience a child as sister, brother, mother, or father. This factor is particularly important in family assessment in a foster-home placement, because the foster child "brings his natural parents with him" (Kaplan, 1953).

Richard Roth, age 11, was placed in a home where the foster parents, the Dawsons, were warm, tender, and considerate; they tried very hard to help Richard feel comfortable and loved. It came as a shock to them when Richard would curse them, demean them, and tell them how horrible they were and how much he wanted to leave their home.

It was not until the social worker, Ms. A, helped the Dawsons realize that Richard was displacing much of the hatred he felt toward his natural parents onto them that they could relate to him with more comfort. Actually Richard felt safer in his foster home and therefore could express his defiance more openly.

As we have suggested several times, because all members of a family are consciously and unconsciously engaged with one another, when one or more members seek out a clinician, this event has meaning for everybody, and they are all consciously and unconsciously participating in it. For example, when Mrs. Smith applies to a social agency so that Tom can attend its summer camp, her request must be assessed not only in terms of the meaning of a vacation to the child, but also with a view toward understanding how the request is experienced by the whole family. What does the request mean to the mother? Does she want to get rid of Tom to give herself a rest? If so, what does this mean to Tom? Do Tom's brothers and sisters feel that he will have an advantage by being at camp? Or do they feel that they will have an advantage? Does Mr. Smith agree that Tom should go to camp?

Dr. Peter Neubauer (1953, p. 115), a psychoanalyst, has stated,

A step forward of one family member may disturb several of the others and could, therefore, create additional disturbances. . . . In making recommendations, the agency that is family-oriented must be aware of the effect of any treatment on the total family. It might at times exclude a procedure which may be helpful to one member of the family, if it would be inadvisable for the family as a whole.

When the clinician utilizes a family focus as part of the assessment and recognizes how the conflicts and presenting problems of one family member invariably involve the other members' participation, the treatment plan will be more comprehensive and will meet the client where he or she is emotionally. Treatment of the school-phobic youngster will take into consideration not only the child's separation anxiety but also the parents' problems. Likewise, treatment of the unmarried mother, the dependent alcoholic, and the antisocial teenager will be enhanced when familial interactions are assessed (Strean, 1979).

CLINICAL CATEGORIES

Inasmuch as clinical categories such as "neurotic," "psychotic," or "character disorder" do not fully describe individuals but tend to stigmatize them and fail to individualize them sufficiently, many clinicians have rejected this form of assessment altogether. Sometimes clinical categories are used in the service of countertransference, as when the practitioner subtly expresses anger or hopelessness by saying: "That borderline [or psychopath, or psychotic] client of mine will never get better." However, inasmuch as terms such as "schizophrenia," "obsessive-compulsive neurotic," or "character disorder" appear frequently in the literature, are utilized in case discussions, and sometimes serve as shortcuts in professional interchanges, it behooves the clinician to have some familiarity with them.

THE NEUROSES

Whenever an individual is suffering from a neurotic symptom such as an obsession or a phobia, psychic conflict is present. The individual's defenses (such as projection and denial), which have been used for protection against ideas, feelings, fantasies, or memories that are unbearable and cause anxiety, have broken down. Anxiety is a warning to the person that some unacceptable drive, thought, or action will reach consciousness. If the unacceptable element is too strong or the defense is too weak, anxiety erupts and the person forms a neurotic symptom. The symptom expresses concomitantly the individual's desire to express a forbidden wish and his or her dread of that expression. In a neurosis expressed by a phobia of going out on the streets, two variables are at work: The very situation that the individual fears also excites him or her. The stimulation that is induced causes anxiety because the excitement emanates from sexual fantasies that are unacceptable to the person. Freud (1923) referred to a neurotic symptom as a "compromise formation" because it is a composite expression of the individual's wishes, anxiety, defenses, and fears.

OBSESSIVE-COMPULSIVE NEUROSIS

The obsessive-compulsive neurotic is tormented by continuous and unwanted thoughts and/or feels compelled to perform certain actions over which he or she has little or no control. Obsessive-compulsive clients are in a constant struggle between strong sadistic wishes and a very powerful need to punish themselves for their "evil" thoughts. The compulsion or obsession is a compromise between two opposing forces: the id's wish to hurt others and the superego's wish for punishment. The ego compromises by forming the obsessive or compulsive symptom.

The person with a hand-washing compulsion must continually clean away his "dirty" thoughts; the man or woman who must constantly check the gas jets is attempting to cope with his or wishes to burn down the house, and the individual who has the obsessive thought "God, strike me dead" is responding to death wishes that he or she has toward people in his or her life, but also wants punishment for these wishes.

The unconscious conflicts in an obsessive-compulsive neurosis deal with problems of love and hate, right and wrong, cleanliness and dirt, orderliness and disorder. Because of the demanding superego in these clients, they suffer from intense guilt (Cameron, 1963).

ANXIETY HYSTERIA

The client suffering from anxiety hysteria experiences pervasive anxiety. Most of the time the anxiety is attached to special objects or situations in the form of phobias—fears of the dark, animals, airplanes, certain foods, and so on. The dreaded object or person usually symbolizes exciting situations. For example, darkness can stimulate forbidden sexual wishes and then create anxiety. To avoid the anxiety, the person avoids dark rooms. Similarly, a certain individual can activate murderous desires in the client. To avoid the anxiety that is engendered by the certain individual, the client avoids the person.

The hysterical client usually suffers from considerable guilt because he or she has strong but unacceptable incestuous and aggressive wishes. The client fears abandonment, death, or mutilation for his or her "sinful" desires. This client also tends to overdramatize emotions and is usually quite exhibitionistic. He or she is usually a person who is very fearful of losing love; consequently, this client is very eager to please others.

The hysterical client has often been, or felt, unacknowledged as a developing sexual boy or girl. He or she attempts as an adult to gratify Oedipal wishes, but guilt and inhibition usually result. The presenting problems of the client with anxiety hysteria may take the form of difficulties in family relationships, in the job situation, or in personal adjustment. The external event that stimulates anxiety usually signifies a sexual or aggressive danger.

CONVERSION HYSTERIA

In conversion hysteria, the client's psychodynamics are quite similar to those of an anxiety hysteric except that symptoms are expressed in a physical form. The physical symptoms give expression to instinctual impulses that have been repressed, and the organ of the body that is chosen expresses the client's specific conflict.

The somatic compliance in conversion hysteria is determined in part by unconscious sexual fantasies and a corresponding erogeneity of the afflicted body part—that is, nongenital zones are "genitalized." Spasms, rhythmical muscular contractions, and sensory disturbances often prove to be simultaneous defenses and substitutes for masturbatory activities.

In sum, the client suffering from conversion hysteria is blocking the expression of sexual impulses. The sexuality dammed up inside expresses itself in unsuitable places and at inconvenient times.

CHARACTER DISORDERS

In contrast to the client with symptomatic neuroses, the client with a character disorder does not suffer from symptoms, but rather expresses his or her conflicts in such character traits as stinginess, demandingness, orderliness, or Don Juan behavior. Whereas the neurotic suffers from *ego-alien* symptoms, the individual with a character disorder induces suffering in others. He or she sees his or her character traits as appropriate ways of coping and will defend their use strenuously. Thus, his or her character traits are *ego-syntonic*.

The client with an *oral character* is one who seeks "mergers" with practically everyone he or she encounters. Although often fed and nurtured as a child, this client has never been successfully weaned. Consequently, the client under discussion has poor impulse control and feels furious or hurt when not immediately gratified. This very narcissistic individual has very limited capacity for autonomy; like a baby, he or she yearns for a symbiotic attachment in order to feel some sense of identity.

The *anal character* is an orderly, frugal, and obstinate person. These traits are partly reaction formations against anal-erotic wishes and partly sublimations of them. Anal character traits express concomitantly a resistance and an obedience to the demands of the environment.

People with a *hysterical character* are usually oversanguine and passionate in their social likes and dislikes, and in their social and sexual relationships they are frequently aggrandizing. Often they are babyish in their emotional contacts, and occasionally they are subject to illusions. Their character traits express a conflict between intense fear of sexuality and strong but repressed sexual strivings. The hysterical character tends to sexualize most "nonsexual" relations and is usually inclined toward suggestibility, irrational emotional outbreaks, chaotic behavior, and histrionics (Fenichel, 1945).

The *psychopath* or *sociopath* is an individual who is constantly fighting inner and outer rules and regulations. He or she abhors the voices of the superego and hates the mandates of society. This individual is unwilling to curb aggressive and sexual impulses because he or she does not feel any obligation to cooperate with an uncooperative world. This client tries to deny guilt but often unconsciously seeks punishment.

The *paranoid character* is always afraid of hidden persecutors. This is a guilt-ridden person who is always anticipating punishment. Frequently, paranoid individuals hate themselves and are constantly ready for an assault from the environment, which they experience as omnipotent and punishing.

SCHIZOPHRENIA

Although there is continual debate about the etiology of schizophrenia, with some experts contending that it is a constitutional defect and others averring that it is an understandable reaction to an impoverished childhood, there is now abundant literature affirming the notion that the schizophrenic client has been deprived of normal physical and emotional stimulation by a maternal figure during the first year of life (Brenner, 1955). In this client, many ego functions have failed to develop properly, and his or her capacity to relate to the external environment is severely impaired—so much so that he or she may even appear feebleminded (Spitz, 1965). The schizophrenic client usually suffers from hallucinations and delusions, distorts reality, is plagued by powerful murderous fantasies that he or she usually projects onto others, and feels that others are out to persecute him or her. Because schizophrenic clients are convinced that most people are their enemies, they withdraw from reality and remain quite seclusive, sometimes talking only to themselves.

Because schizophrenic clients withdraw libido (energy) from other people and direct it toward themselves, they feel estranged, depersonalized, and preoccupied with body sensations. Their regression to or fixation at a very infantile, narcissistic state accounts for their megalomania; they sometimes fantasy that they are somebody very special, such as an emperor or a queen.

Erikson (1950) has described the schizophrenic individual as one who has either lost or never gained a basic sense of trust and therefore has to resort to a narcissistic, paranoid orientation to the world. The thinking of this individual falls back from the logical to the prelogical level, and he or she is consumed by archaic wishes that gives rise to hallucinatory and delusional thinking.

Just as the differences between a "normal" individual and a neurotic are a matter of degree, it can be said that the differences between a schizophrenic individual and a neurotic are also a matter of degree. Precipitating factors in neuroses and schizophrenia are similar and only quantitative. In schizophrenia, anxiety is more overwhelming than it is for the neurotic and it becomes terror; the terror floods the ego, and ego functions are therefore grossly impaired.

MANIC-DEPRESSIVE PSYCHOSES

Similar to schizophrenic clients, manic-depressives are extremely narcissistic and infantile, have minimal emotional investment in others, have lost many ego functions, and frequently depart from reality. One of the unique characteristics of manic-depressive clients is their rapid alteration of moods. They can shift from intense joy to acute depression within an hour.

The mood swings in manic-depressive individuals seem to mirror a situation in which the baby is alternately abandoned and then loved intensely, only to be abandoned again. Differing from schizophrenic clients who seem to have suffered from a great deal of estrangement, manic-depressives appear to be products of very tempestuous, unpredictable environments that offered much pain but also sporadic pleasure.

The exaggerated self-love of the manic-depressive client during the manic phase is often accompanied by a flight of ideas. It is as if the client is desperately holding on to a joyful state but wondering when the mother's comfort will be withdrawn (Glover, 1949). In the depressive phase of the psychosis, one can usually see that the client has suffered decisive narcissistic injuries. The client has severe and agitated crying jags and seems like a child who is tremendously disappointed in the parents for not loving him or her (Fenichel, 1945).

The manic-depressive client seems to be continually alternating between hunger and satiety. Pleasure is expected after every pain, and pain after every pleasure. The primitive idea is set up that any suffering bestows the privilege of some later compensating joy, and vice versa (Fenichel, 1945).

BORDERLINE AND SCHIZOID STATES

Individuals who do not manifest a true psychosis but function at a trust-mistrust, or oral, level of development, have been variously referred to as borderline, schizoid, ambulatory schizophrenic, and pseudoneurotic schizophrenic. Although these clients frequently suffer from the extreme narcissism, feelings of omnipotence, lack of true interpersonal relationships, departures from reality, and poor judgment associated with psychosis, they usually have some ego functions that are working well, at least at certain times. Sometimes they can use good judgment on a job but are unrelated in a marriage, or vice versa. They may be extremely preoccupied with their bodies but manage to function for periods of time in a symptom-free manner. These individuals have not broken with reality, yet under unfavorable circumstances they can become psychotic (Fenichel, 1945; Glover, 1949).

Kaufman (1958) has pointed out that the "borderline personality" can be characterized as having (1) many overt depressions, (2) an inability to handle many of the realities of living, (3) a tendency to act out (delinquency, alcoholism, or addiction), (4) psychosomatic reactions, and (5) paranoid reactions. Kaufman has further pointed out that the borderline personality uses a great deal of magical thinking. Often, if he or she gets into difficulty, there is the belief that a parental figure will come to the rescue.

ADDICTIONS

Either because they have not been given appropriate love and attention or because higher levels of development have created too much anxiety for them to master and then they regress, the drug addict, food addict, heavy smoker, and alcoholic are all trying to satisfy a strong emotional hunger. Once the yearning is satisfied, these individuals feel a temporary sense of security and self-esteem.

Inasmuch as the addict frequently feels distrustful of people, he or she resorts to the solitary pleasure of the addiction rather than depending on interpersonal relationships for gratification. The drug, alcohol, or food that addicts constantly ingest is experienced as equivalent to the warmth and comfort which they crave from a mother but which they must consciously repudiate.

Berthelsdorf (1976) has called attention to the strength of these clients' omnipotent fantasies. When they are on a "high," they feel that they can control the world. However, these individuals also have many unconscious passive wishes and a strong conviction that they are basically weak individuals. They try to surmount these feelings through imbibing drugs or alcohol.

PSYCHOSOMATIC DISEASE

Most people are aware of physiological accompaniments to various emotions. If a person is angry, he or she may find himself or herself breathing quickly, perspiring, and trembling. Loving feelings are often accompanied by fast heartbeats and other visceral sensations. It is apparent that undischarged quantities of anger can lead to a migraine headache or insomnia; unfulfilled dependency wishes that are forbidden and cause anxiety can lead to an ulcer, and undischarged and frustrated libidinal longings can induce heart conditions.

There is some controversy regarding the unconscious meaning of psychosomatic illness. Some authors contend that they are merely expressions of dammed-up excitation and tension and do not express a unique set of conflicts (Glover, 1949). Others have concluded that a part of the body is unconsciously selected to express a unique psychological conflict (Fenichel, 1945). Those who subscribe to the view that a particular bodily dysfunction, such as bronchial asthma, expresses a unique conflict would point out that an asthmatic seizure might be interpreted as an intense longing for a mother and as a desperate cry for help. They would avow that dermatitis could be viewed as crying out through the skin and that colitis might express the wish to withhold defiant feelings.

The clinician working with an individual who has a psychosomatic problem frequently observes a diminution of symptoms when the client is given the opportunity to talk about what the "grinding stomach" or "heavy heart" is saying. When the person who complains of a heart pain or stomach ache is given a chance to speak about his or her psychological conflict, the pain tends to lessen (Deutsch, 1953).

Psychosomatic reactions are frequently accommodations that have been made in childhood, and the same somatic reactions can continue into adult life.

SEXUAL DISORDERS

Inasmuch as so many patterns of "unconventional" sexual behavior have gained much acceptance in recent years, many clinicians and nonclinicians have been reluctant to examine their dynamic meanings. Some seem to feel that seeking to unravel the unconscious meanings of such practices as homosexuality or celibacy or other forms of nontraditional sexual behavior is evidence of arrogance or intolerance.

To the psychodynamically oriented practitioner, the client's overt sexual behavior is much less crucial than how he or she experiences himself or herself with partners in and out of bed. As with any form of behavior, the psychodynamic clinician wants to learn what fantasies stimulate anxiety, how punitive is the superego, and what is the client's capacity for empathy.

Sex is much more than a bodily experience; it is also an interpersonal transaction. It is our contention that people who have successfully resolved the maturational conflicts of trust versus mistrust, autonomy versus doubt, initiative versus guilt, and so on, will be capable of enjoying, and will want to receive the gratification from, a full sexual and interpersonal relationship with a member of the opposite sex. However, if they cannot *trust*, they will be suspicious of a partner; if they cannot feel *autonomous*, they will be enormously frightened in a sexual relationship; and if they cannot take initiative, they will be burdened by much anxiety in asserting their sexual roles (Strean, 1983).

In male *impotence*, the man frequently equates his sexual partner with his mother and feels guilty about his incestuous fantasies and competitive thoughts. To avoid the anxiety that accrues from these fantasies and thoughts, he withdraws from sex. Frequently, the impotent man feels very hostile toward women and unconsciously fears a battle, so he withdraws. Many men are unconsciously envious of women and, to avoid facing their rivalry and their wishes to be a woman themselves, stop themselves from enjoying sex.

The *frigid* woman may also be unconsciously equating her sexual partner with the parent of the opposite sex and then punishing herself for her rivalry with her mother. Frequently the woman who does not enjoy sex with a man is in competition with him and would like to mutilate him. Feeling frightened of her hostility and envious of her partner, she cannot enjoy him.

While all human beings have desires to be members of the opposite sex, and while biological factors such as hormonal balance contribute toward a particular sexual orientation, there is now abundant evidence that men and women who have exclusive sex with members of their same gender have experienced very ungratifying childhoods, are filled with much rage and self-doubt, and suffer from enormous anxiety. Their homosexuality, according to psychodynamic theory, is a regression to ward off frightening fantasies and feared punishment (Fine, 1981; Socarides, 1978; Strean, 1983).[1] Similar statements can be made about bisexuality and transvestism.

In completing our review of clinical categories, we would like to reiterate that diagnostic labels have many limitations. First, they are not mutually exclusive; for example, one can see a hysterical character who also has many unresolved oral wishes, or one can see a paranoid person who also has severe sexual problems. Second, clinical categories do not usually give us a real understanding of the client's psychic structure and its interaction with the environment; the understanding is usually quite superficial. Finally, instead of individualizing an assessment, clinical categories can serve to stigmatize and stereotype the client and serve the purpose of gratifying countertransference problems.

NOTE

1. Of all the topics included in a discussion of sexual disorders, homosexuality is most contentious in current practice. As the reader is well aware, there are many points of view regarding the etiology of homosexuality. The orientation espoused here is a psychoanalytic one.

REFERENCES

Adler, G. (1967). Methods of treatment in analytical psychology. In B. Wolman (Ed.), *Psychoanalytic techniques*. New York: Basic Books.

Bertalanffy, L. (1968). *General systems theory*. New York: George Braziller.

Berthelsdorf, S. (1976). Survey of the successful analysis of a young man addicted to heroin. In K. Eissler (Ed.), *The psychoanalytic study of the child* (Vol. 31). New Haven, CT: Yale University Press.

Borenzweig, H. (1971). Social work and psychoanalytic theory. *Social Work, 16*(1).

Brenner, C. (1955). *An elementary textbook of psychoanalysis*. New York: International Universities Press.

Briar, S., & Miller, H. (1971). *Problems and issues in social casework*. New York: Columbia University Press.

Buckley, W. (1967). *Sociology and modern systems theory*. Englewood Cliffs, NJ: Prentice-Hall.

Cameron, N. (1963). *Personality development and psychopathology*. Boston: Houghton Mifflin.

Compton, B., & Galaway, B. (1975). *Social work processes*. Homewood, IL: Irwin.

Deutsch, F. (1953). The application of psychoanalysis to psychomatic aspects of social work. In M. Heiman (Ed.), *Psychoanalysis and social work*. New York: International Universities Press.

Eisenstein, V. (1956). Sexual problems in marriage. In V. Eisenstein (Ed.), *Neurotic interaction in marriage*. New York: Basic Books.

Erikson, E. (1950). *Childhood and society*. New York: Norton.

Fenichel, O. (1945). *The psychoanalytic theory of neuroses.* New York: Norton.

Fine, R. (1981). *The psychoanalytic vision.* New York: Free Press.

Fine, R. (1979). *A history of psychoanalysis.* New York: Columbia University Press.

Fine, R. (1973). Psychoanalysis. In R. Corsini (Ed.), *Current psychotherapies.* Itasca, IL: Peacock.

Fisher, J. (1976). *The effectiveness of social casework.* Springfield, IL: Charles C Thomas.

Freud, A. (1973). *The ego and the mechanisms of defense.* London: Hogarth Press.

Freud, S. (1939). *An outline of psychoanalysis.* London: Hogarth Press.

Freud, S. (1938). *The basic writings of Sigmund Freud.* New York: Random House.

Freud, S. (1923). *The ego and the id.* London: Hogarth Press.

Glover, E. (1949). *Psychoanalysis.* London: Staples Press.

Hall, C., & Lindzey, G. (1957). *Theories of personality.* London: John Wiley.

Hamilton, G. (1958). A theory of personality: Freud's contribution to social work. In H. Parad (Ed.), *Ego psychology and dynamic casework.* New York: Family Services Association of America.

Hamilton, G. (1951). *Theory and practice of social casework.* New York: Columbia University Press.

Hartmann, H. (1964). *Essays on ego psychology.* New York: International Universities Press.

Hartmann, H. (1951). *Ego psychology and the problem of adaptation.* New York: International Universities Press.

Hollis, F. (1972). *Casework: A psychosocial therapy* (2nd ed.). New York: Random House.

Hollis, F. (1964). *Casework: A psychosocial therapy* (1st ed.). New York: Random House.

Jackson, D. (1957). The question of family homeostasis. *Psychiatric Quarterly, 31.*

Kaplan, L. (1953). Foster home placement. In M. Heiman (Ed.), *Psychoanalysis and social work.* New York: International Universities Press.

Kaufman, I. (1958). Therapeutic considerations in the borderline personality structure. In H. Parad (Ed.), *Ego psychology and dynamic casework.* New York: Family Services Association of America.

Langs, R. (1981). *Resistances and interventions.* New York: Jason Aronson.

Mahoney, K., & Mahoney, M. (1974). Psychoanalytic guidelines for child placement. *Social Work, 19*(6).

Neubauer, P. (1953). The psychoanalyst's contribution to the family agency. In M. Heiman (Ed.), *Psychoanalysis and social work.* New York: International Universities Press.

Richmond, M. (1917). *Social diagnosis.* New York: Russell Sage Foundation.

Rosenblatt, A. (1961). The application of role concepts to the intake process. *Social Casework, 43.*

Ruesch, J. (1961). *Therapeutic communication.* New York: Norton.

Socarides, C. (1978). *Homosexuality.* New York: Jason Aronson.

Spiegel, J. (1960). The resolution of role conflict with the family. In N. Bell and E. Vogel (Eds.), *The family.* New York: Free Press.

Spitz, R. (1965). *The first year of life.* New York: International Universities Press.

Stanton, A., & Schwartz, M. (1954). *The mental hospital.* New York: Basic Books.

Stein, I. (1971). The systems model and social systems theory: Their application to social casework. In H. Strean (Ed.), *Social casework: Theories in action.* Metuchen, NJ: Scarecrow Press.

Strean, H. (1985). *Resolving marital conflicts.* New York: John Wiley.
Strean, H. (1983). *The sexual dimension.* New York: Free Press.
Strean, H. (1979). *Psychoanalytic theory and social work practice.* New York: Free Press.
Strean, H. (1978). *Clinical social work.* New York: Free Press.
Strean, H. (1970). A family therapist looks at Little Hans. In H. Strean (Ed.), *New approaches in child guidance.* Metuchen, NJ: Scarecrow Press.
Zilbach, J. (1968). Family development. In J. Marmor (Ed.), *Modern psychoanalysis.* New York: Basic Books.

Chapter 3

THE TREATMENT PLAN

Having made a comprehensive psychosocial assessment of the client and of his or her situation, the practitioner is ready to plan treatment; that is, the practitioner is ready to specify with and for the client individualized goals for improved psychosocial functioning.

It is important to keep in mind that planning treatment is never an isolated activity. From the very first contact with the client, when practitioners are gathering data, they are also working toward an assessment. Throughout the life of any case, the practitioner is concomitantly gathering data, making assessments, and attempting to utilize these assessments to formulate a treatment plan. However, for purposes of discussion, we are separating these processes but are bearing in mind that the more data that are gathered, the better is the psychosocial assessment, and the more comprehensive the assessment is, the more refined and individualized the treatment plan will be (Richmond, 1917; Hamilton, 1951; Strean, 1978).

Treatment planning is a deliberate, rational process involving designs for action calculated to achieve specific objectives at some future time (Hamilton, 1951; Perlman & Gurin, 1972). It is concerned with moving from problem definition to problem solution, from knowing what is socially and psychologically disruptive to the client to becoming aware of what is to be done, how, by whom, and in what sequence. The treatment plan frequently has goals for immediate, intermediate, and long-term change. It may shift during the course of treatment interviews or even during a single interview as the practitioner and client become aware of new data in the client's past, present, or future interactions and transactions.

Particularly in social work, but in other disciplines as well, a treatment plan may involve others in addition to the client and the practitioner. For example, work with an individual might require intervention in the family system, and work with a family might require some work with the individuals alone. The client's motivation, his or her capacities, his or her opportunities (Ripple, Alexander, & Polemis, 1964), and his or her degree of discomfort with the current person-situation constellation will influence the scope and the complexity of the treatment plan. Also, how willing the individual is to be a client will certainly shape the treatment plan.

THE CLIENT'S RIGHT
TO SELF-DETERMINATION

Planning treatment and positing goals for clients have raised questions in the minds of some practitioners. If one genuinely believes in the importance of self-determination for a client, can one really *plan* treatment *for* the client? For example, many psychodynamically oriented therapists have "the analytic ideal" (Fine, 1981) in mind as they establish goals for and with their clients. This ideal posits that the therapist should try to help clients to reduce their hatred and increase their capacity to love; to have realistic pleasure, to enjoy a full sexual life, to be able to communicate, to experience a wide variety of emotions, to have a role in the family and in the society and be devoid of symptoms. However, there are probably few, if any, clients who seek out therapists with "the analytic ideal" in mind. Most clients want quick relief from their distress and are not much interested in any long-term treatment plan.

Yet, as we observed in Chapters 1 and 2, when the practitioner explores clients' requests in depth, the latter's views toward their problems do change and their fantasies about the helping process are altered. What is important to keep in mind as we try to respect our clients' right to self-determination is that treatment plans are always made mutually with the client. If a treatment plan does not meet the needs and wishes of the client, he or she will communicate this to the practitioner by exhibiting some form of resistance—coming to interviews late, canceling appointments, refusing to talk, not paying fees, and so on. These behaviors and the feelings that propel them must be related to in the treatment plan if the helping process is going to be successful.

The practitioner can try to stimulate clients to think about themselves and their relationships, but only the clients themselves can do it. The practitioner has the responsibility of deciding what form of help will be *offered,* but clients exercise control over what they accept. No form of intervention can be successful if the client does not want to participate in it.

After Norman and Eleanor Adams had several interviews with Mr. Z, a marriage counselor, Mr. Z suggested that he see each of the Adamses separately once a week, and the two of them together every other week. While Mr. Z explained to the Adamses that each of them had difficulty providing the other with some space, and that was why he recommended individual treatment primarily, the strong symbiotic relationship that characterized the Adamses' marriage was threatened by his treatment plan and they both balked. Mr. Z, after recognizing the acute separation anxiety that Norman and Eleanor were experiencing, felt compelled to rescind his suggestion and continued to see them exclusively in conjoint marital counseling.

If potential clients do not appear to be highly motivated to participate in a treatment plan because they fear exposure, feel too much or too little distress about their problems, are pessimistic about their solution, or hold certain values which discourage their participation in a helping process, these issues must themselves be aired, explored, and understood by the practitioner; they should be considered immediate issues for the treatment plan (Hellenbrand, 1961).

As we will recall from our discussion in Chapters 1 and 2, clients have feelings about their referral sources, they may define their problems superficially, or they may deny that they even exist. These very important issues deserve the highest priority in any treatment plan. If they are not given the priority they deserve, treatment will be disrupted.

Joan and Arthur Bernstein brought their 10-year-old son, David, to a child guidance clinic for help with his learning difficulties and his poor peer relationships. Although the social worker, Ms. Y, made a thorough study of David's difficulties, his history, and the Bernsteins's family background, she told Joan and Arthur as they were leaving at the end of their second interview that they would be seen at the clinic every other week. Because the Bernsteins were not interested in being seen for themselves, they pulled David out of therapy. Had they been more tactfully pursued and given some time to consider whether they wanted to participate in a treatment plan, they might not have abandoned Ms. Y so quickly.

INTERVENTIVE PLANS CONCERNING
THE CLIENT'S SOCIAL SITUATION

We have constantly stressed that our approach to clients in distress is "psychosocial." Just as the assessment always considers the person and situation as interdependent and consistently focuses on the interaction between situational variables and personality dynamics, the treatment plan always has a similar perspective. One cannot make a treatment plan for Mr. Jones without considering its impact on his family, job, spouse, and so on. By the same token, the practitioner cannot intervene in Mr. Jones's environment without considering its impact on him, personally.

When helping professionals sense the discomfort clients experience in an oppressive environment, they are frequently tempted to make this issue number one on the treatment agenda and move in to correct the unwholesome situation immediately. Unfortunately, many clients cannot easily accept quick alteration of their current situation, no matter how disturbing it is. As we pointed out in Chapter 2, client and situation have evolved through mutually adaptive transactions over time. Consequently, a self-hating, depressed person can feel strong anxiety when a nicer home, better meals, or more caring relationships are offered. The social situation of a client, no matter how disruptive it is, mirrors the client's self-image. Therefore, before goods or services are assigned a top priority in the treatment plan, part of the plan should include some discussion between helper and helpee on how the latter experiences being given to. Exploration of this item on the treatment plan's agenda usually helps involve the client in treatment when he or she has an opportunity to pour out ambivalent, angry, and distrustful feelings about being helped.

It is extremely important when planning intervention in the environment of impoverished clients to remember that many of these clients do not trust the helper. Consequently, in helping a client who is depressed, mistrustful, and living in an oppressive environment, frequently the first item on the interventive agenda is to help the client discuss his or her distrust of the agency and the worker.

Saul Cousins, an 8-year-old boy living in a slum, initially accepted a referral to a community center by Mr. W, a social worker; however, he never attended one session, although he was eager to do so. It was later learned that Saul thought Mr. W was a truant officer and could not trust him. When this issue was clarified, Saul could accept the referral.

TREATMENT PLANNING AND THE CLIENT'S LIFE-TASKS

As we briefly discussed in Chapter 2 when we referred to Erikson (1950) and ego psychology, one way of conceptualizing assessment is to pinpoint the one or more life-tasks with which clients are not able to cope. Clients, as we suggested, have either regressed to or are fixated at trust versus mistrust, autonomy versus self-doubt, initiative versus guilt, and so on. In planning treatment, the clinician can ask himself or herself, "Which life-tasks does this client need to resolve better, and how will I go about trying to help the client do this?"

In commenting about life-tasks, Erikson has postulated a "radius of significant others" in the person's social orbit—spouses, parents, teachers, friends, extended family, and the like—who can aid, abet, or hinder the resolution of a life-task. For example, a child who needs to learn to trust needs a trustworthy maternal figure who will offer tenderness, love, care, and availability. By the same token, a client who is full of distrust needs a humane and caring professional to help him or her overcome distrust and develop some inner certainty. Therefore, clinicians in planning treatment can conceive of their own roles as key significant others who, through their attitudes, skills, and efforts, help clients move up the psychosocial ladder and resolve life-tasks. Clinicians may also view themselves as catalysts who help significant others in the client's environment to enact roles so that the client's psychological and interpersonal functioning can be enhanced.

Let us recall Erikson's life-tasks and show how the nature of these tasks can provide certain guides for planning treatment.

TRUST VERSUS MISTRUST CONFLICTS

Clients showing a high ratio of mistrust to trust usually are and have been individuals who have been psychologically, socially, economically, or physically neglected. Often they are the products of broken homes who have had impoverished interactions with depressed or ill parents. Usually these clients emerge as affectless and depressed and frequently are paranoid. They may be acute alcoholics, chronic schizophrenics, abusive parents, or tyrannical spouses. In this category are also clients who are chronically unemployed. Many times they are on public assistance and live in very oppressive environments.

In planning treatment for these clients, in most cases they need one-to-one, long-term treatment. However, because these clients are so distrustful, they will distrust the practitioner. Therefore, the initial treatment goal with them is to help them verbalize and to verbalize for them their suspicion of the helping process and of the helper and their anger at being helped. Part of the treatment plan with these clients is also to help them with their wishes to test the helper. This requires an attitude of persistence on the part of the clinician, who should not lose faith in the client or in the helping process when the former cancels appointments, has nothing to say in interviews, or becomes pessimistic about treatment.

When the practitioner can form a relationship with the client which permits the client to verbalize anger and distrust, the client's self-esteem, inner certainty, and confidence in the practitioner usually rise. Then the client is usually more receptive to intervention in his or her environment, and the aid of landlords, teachers, and policemen, and the like can be enlisted.

Treatment with the client who has trust-mistrust conflicts is usually very difficult but very rewarding. If clinicians constantly keep in mind that much of their effort involves helping such clients to voice distrust toward them (and toward others) without censoring them or without retaliating when they are provocative, these clients can grow.

In working with Ms. Pauline Diamond, age 32, a mother on welfare with three children, Ms. V, the social worker at a mental health center, recognized that Pauline had many personal and social problems which needed a carefully constructed treatment plan. Pauline was an acute alcoholic she was constantly unemployed and on public welfare, she had been through three marriages during a period of nine years, she was in frequent physical and verbal fights with her children, her house was run-down, and she and the children were not eating or sleeping properly.

Reviewing her history, Ms. V learned that Pauline's mother had died when Pauline was a year and a half old. She had little contact with her father and went from foster home to foster home, never feeling loved or comforted at any of these places. Her school record was poor, and her social relationships were very thin.

Inasmuch as Ms. V saw that Pauline was very guarded in her relationship with her, the client's suspicions of help and the helper became the first item on the therapeutic agenda. When Pauline's ambivalence toward help was discussed with her and some of her lifelong hostility was released, Pauline could then reveal to Ms. V some of her yearnings for a parent. While Ms. V realized that Pauline's intense hostility and deep desire for nurturance would always be part of the treatment, as the client became more trusting of her therapist, she could eventually accept a homemaker, guidance in child rearing, and some help with her sexual and interpersonal problems with men.

Although Ms. V had planned initially to see Pauline in once-a-week treatment, as their relationship deepened it was necessary for Ms. V to see Pauline two or three times weekly.

AUTONOMY VERSUS SHAME AND DOUBT CONFLICTS

There are two groups of clients whose life-tasks center on the conflict of autonomy versus shame and doubt. First, there are those clients who have little confidence in their own capacities and limited faith in their significant others, because they have been expected to do too much too soon on their own. Prematurely forced into autonomy too early in life and/or finding themselves in jobs or other situations that burdened them with too much responsibility, these clients are often depressed, overwhelmed, and suffer from somatic ills such as migraine headaches or insomnia. In this category are the frightened and compulsive student, the harassed mother or father, or the workaholic man or woman. In the second group are those clients who have been insufficiently encouraged to perform with some autonomy, independence, and concern for others. Here we have the overdemanding parent or child, the rebellious adolescent or adult, or the chronically complaining spouse. These are all clients who cling to passivity because they have not learned to be active on their own behalf.

In helping clients who are responding to perfectionistic standards which are usually internal as well as external, the form of help that seems most appropriate for them is one-to-one treatment (occasionally group or family treatment can be the modality of choice) whereby these clients will receive permission and encouragement to relax controls and to lessen overwhelming standards. These clients need a therapist who will be a benign superego and who will help them give up defenses against assertion and spontaneity—things that they very much fear.

Roy Erikson was an 11-year-old boy who was referred for help because he was daydreaming in class, was inattentive at both home and school, and was very phobic. In making his assessment, Mr. U, his therapist, recognized that Roy was very much pushed by his parents to achieve and felt overwhelmed by all that was imposed on him. He seemed to be the type of child who believed that the only way he could be loved was to produce. Unable to vent his hostility, he daydreamed and passively rebelled.

In formulating his treatment plan, Mr. U reasoned that Roy would probably feel compelled to produce for him. Therefore, he tried to establish a very permissive atmosphere in the play therapy with Roy. If Roy could not enjoy himself "just playing," Mr. U would try to help him see how frightened he was to relax and how terrified he was to oppose internalized sanctions. Finger painting, eating food, and similar activities would help Roy learn that life and relationships could consist of more than hard work.

In addition to the above plan, Roy's parents were involved in the treatment plan. They were people who felt very pressured, and part of the plan with them was to help them loosen their inner and outer controls.

In making an interventive plan for clients who have been indulged, clinicians should conceive of their role as that of "trainer." Here, limits should be set when the client acts impulsively and praise can be offered when the client shows some self-control and some autonomy. The clinician should also attempt to influence significant others in the client's environment so that they will provide the kinds of attitudes and relationships that the clinician is attempting to provide.

Sally Frankel, age 19, was a college student referred to the student mental health center because she was failing her courses, was belligerent toward peers and professors, was on drugs, and in many ways was "the college rebel."

Assessing her person-situation constellation, Ms. T, her therapist, concluded that Sally was the product of an overpermissive, indulgent home. As a result, Sally was very narcissistic and insensitive to others.

In formulating her treatment plan, Ms. T felt that Sally needed a corrective emotional experience in the treatment relationship. Because Sally was very demanding, Ms. T would not gratify her demands but instead would ask her what she was feeling when Sally asked questions of her or insisted upon getting certain responses from her. When Sally denigrated other people, Ms. T would try to help her see what childish wishes Sally was trying to gratify. When Sally would come late to appointments, Ms. T would ask her about her contemptuous feelings toward her. Also, Sally's significant others would be helped not to indulge her. Discussions would be held with dormitory heads and others, with Sally's permission.

INITIATIVE VERSUS GUILT CONFLICTS

Clients who have difficulty enjoying their sexual roles are experiencing anxiety about taking initiative and feel very guilty when they do so. In their minds, assertiveness in general, but particularly sexual assertiveness, appears to be a hostile act; consequently, they repress their spontaneity and are very inhibited. Married couples with sexual problems fit into this category, along with single people who are frightened of intimate, heterosexual relationships. In this category are also children and adults who fear success. They fail in school or on the job because they distort the meaning of achievements and think of them as vengeful acts which should be punished.

These clients can be seen in individual, dyadic, family, or group treatment, depending on their own wishes and ego capacities. The main thing the practitioner should try to do with them is to help them look at and talk about their sexual fantasies and their aggressive wishes. These clients need an atmosphere in which initiative is championed and repression is questioned, in which verbalization of feelings and thoughts is encouraged and in which childish fantasies are tolerated. These clients also need to be helped to differentiate between fantasies and reality. Often when they have incestuous or hostile fantasies, they cannot differentiate between wishes and deeds and tend to believe they are perverted psychopaths. In effect, these clients have regressed to or are fixated at an Oedipal level, and they do not recognize that Oedipal wishes are universal phenomena. They need much help in order to see that if they assert themselves toward authority, they are not killing the authority, and that if they experience their spouses as parental figures, they are not participating in active incest.

As suggested, these clients tend to do well in most treatment modalities, providing they experience the atmosphere as permissive and warm.

Diane and Morton Green, a couple in their early thirties, were being seen by Mr. S for marriage counseling. Although they had been married for four years, they had participated in sex only about six times.

In assessing the Greens, Mr. S was able to learn that both of the Greens came from homes where sexuality and intimacy were repudiated. Both Diane and Morton tended to view sex, therefore, as a rebellious act.

In formulating a treatment plan, Mr. S decided on conjoint marriage counseling whereby the Greens would be encouraged to share with each other and with Mr. S their rebellious fantasies. As the Greens were given permission to rebel in fantasy and saw that no damage to anyone resulted, they could trust themselves much more in sex.

Although the Greens were seen in conjoint treatment, it was necessary to shift the treatment plan. When it became clear to Mr. S and to the Greens themselves that Diane and Morton each had certain sexual and aggressive fantasies that were difficult to discuss in front of each other, the plan shifted to one-to-one individual treatment for both.

In working with individuals whose problems center on initiative versus guilt, clinicians have found that many of these clients have many ego functions intact and are quite well motivated to do therapeutic work. In addition to helping them face forbidden sexual and aggressive fantasies, which they are often able to do within an empathetic therapeutic relationship, these clients also need to be encouraged to take on tasks in their environment. These people often do respond well when asked why they cannot ask the boss for a raise or why they cannot go to a movie or partake in some other type of recreation (Austin, 1958).

INDUSTRY VERSUS INFERIORITY CONFLICTS

In this category are clients who tend to feel that their peers, colleagues, and virtually everyone around them are superior to them. Frightened to assert themselves and suffering from low self-esteem, they often lead constricted lives. The school-phobic child, the young adult who suffers from social anxiety, the older adult who fears entering into new social situations—are all part of this group.

Clients who suffer from an inability to be industrious can often profit from social or therapy groups in which the professional leader does not permit too much dependency on himself or herself. Rather, the group leader encourages these clients to seek solutions from other members, helps them to understand their inhibitions in asking for things, and assists them in facing their fears of intimacy. The practitioner tries to help these clients acquire, through group interaction, the interpersonal skills that they cannot seem to achieve in their constricted environments, which seem to squelch their attempts at industrious behavior. The practitioner also attempts to help these clients, when they feel stronger, to try to modify their environments when they can.

Tom Heft, a 25-year-old man who feared group situations, requested group therapy, which the social worker at the family agency, Mr. R, agreed to arrange. Tom was a constricted man who found it difficult to assert himself with peers but was overdependent on authorities. As Mr. R saw this tendency of Tom's recapitulated in the therapy group, a treatment plan was formulated to help Tom try to resolve this immature pattern. When Tom sought out Mr. R by asking him questions and requesting his advice, Mr. R turned to the group members and asked them how they were experiencing Tom as he clung to Mr. R. As a result, the group members and Tom were stimulated into interactions and trans-actions—the very thing that Tom feared in his everyday life. Continual discussions between the group members and Tom helped him become much more industrious, which considerably reduced his strong inferiority feelings. As Tom felt more comfortable with himself and with the group members, he was helped by the latter to move into a better apartment in a better neighborhood.

IDENTITY VERSUS ROLE DIFFUSION CONFLICTS

Social and therapeutic groups are often helpful to clients who have difficulty knowing their own strengths, values, skills, and limitations. Individuals who are still not sure whether they are children or adults, or clients who are entering into a new role, such as a parenting role, supervisor, or new member of a community, all wonder who they are and what the new and different expectations of them really are.

In formulating a treatment plan for these clients, the clinician tries to provide a group for them so that members can discuss their conflicting role expectations, uncertain values, and frightening tasks.

When Rose Isaacs, age 36, became a supervisor in her office, she was very frightened of assuming authority because all of her life she had felt "like an underling" or "like a child." Ms. Q, the group therapist, planned several things for Rose in the group, all of which were quite helpful to her. Often Ms. Q would turn to Rose and ask her what she thought the group members were really thinking and feeling. She also helped Rose to direct and to advise others in the group, and Ms. Q, at times, tried to stimulate interaction between Rose and members of the group who were in managerial, executive, and supervisory positions.

All of the aforementioned dimensions of Ms. Q's treatment plan for Rose were planned experiences which served as "dress rehearsals" for Rose in assuming her new role of supervisor.

INTIMACY VERSUS ISOLATION CONFLICTS

In this category are clients who have anxiety about intimate interpersonal relationships, usually with both sexes. These are people who often fail in marriage, in friendships, and in love affairs. They tend to see loving as an entrapment and closeness as a loss of individuality. Inasmuch as one-to-one relationships frighten them, they are best served professionally in a one-to-one long-term relationship. However, some of these people reject one-to-one treatment and may have to start being helped in a group. Often a group experience can motivate them to accept individual treatment later.

In the one-to-one treatment relationship, the practitioner should try to help these clients face their fears of feeling close to the practitioner and learn what really immobilizes them.

Mitchell Johnson, age 40, had been through two marriages and a host of unsuccessful love affairs. Every time he got close to a woman, he would become very critical of her and reject her. Ms. P, his therapist, sensitive to this pattern of Mitchell's, told him in his second interview with her that sooner or later, he would want to reject her. When he felt like doing so, it would be very helpful if he could come in to his sessions and discuss these wishes with Ms. P.

Because Mitchell felt very much understood and protected by Ms. P, he was able to see that this criticism of women was a defense to protect himself against strong fears of being dominated by them, because unconsciously he made women the tyrannical mother of his past.

When the practitioner notes a consistent dysfunctional behavioral pattern of a client early in the contact, it is often a good idea to warn the client that this pattern is bound to emerge in the therapeutic relationship. This kind of therapeutic planning, as shown in the above case situation with Mitchell Johnson, is often very reassuring to clients because they feel protected and less overwhelmed when they begin to flounder in therapy.

As the client who fears intimacy studies this fear in the helper-helpee relationship and sees how he or she unconsciously arranges rejection, the client is usually more enabled to resolve this life-task and take on intimate relationships with others in more comfort.

GENERATIVITY VERSUS STAGNATION CONFLICTS

When clients begin to get older and are compelled to cope with physical, intellectual, and other limitations, they often become bitter and feel deprived and rejected. They are frequently anxious and self-conscious when with their own children or grandchildren. In this category are the angry boss, the frightened parent of a teenager, and the threatened teacher or supervisor. These clients frequently fear the loss of their powers and the loss of their identities.

If these clients are parents, they can often derive benefit from family treatment. Also, group treatment in which the members have similar difficulties can be helpful. The majority of these clients, however, profit a great deal from a one-to-one treatment relationship with a younger person who encourages them to talk about their real achievements as well as their real losses. Feeling respected and encouraged by one whom they think is ready to reject them can be very therapeutic for them.

George King, a retired man in his seventies and a widower, was very depressed. Although he had accomplished a great deal in his life, he had become very self-effacing and thought he had "nothing to live for."

After assessing his personality and situation carefully, Mr. C, his social worker, planned to help Mr. King talk about his many achievements in the therapy. As he did so, Mr. C would try to help Mr. King utilize some of his strengths in the present. When it came out that Mr. King had been a Boy Scout leader in his youth, Mr. C helped his client become a leader in a children's center. When it turned out that Mr. King had done a lot of square dancing, he discussed with his client becoming a caller at dances. While many resistances of Mr. King had to be aired, feeling respected and accepted by Mr. C lessened his feeling of stagnation and helped to regenerate him.

EGO INTEGRITY VERSUS DESPAIR

Often similar to clients who feel they are stagnating, clients in this category frequently suffer from a great deal of self-hatred. They question the contributions they have made to the world and often berate themselves. In contrast to clients in the preceding category, who often respond to encouragement rather soon, the clients in this category, because they are very depressed, desperate, and sometimes even suicidal, resist the helper for some time.

Often clients in this category have been shunned by their families and extended families, who resent their frequent complaints about physical and psychological aches and pains. These clients are often placed in homes for the aged and forgotten. As a result, their feelings of isolation and self-hatred are very strong.

Because clients in this category are very depressed, they need the patience, persistence, and faith of one person who will not give up on them and will see them frequently for interviews. Usually these clients need much help in verbalizing their hatred and hurt toward those whom they feel have abandoned them. When this is done successfully, they often can participate in their environment with more integrity.

Lucy Lyons, age 80, was in a home for the aged and spent most of her time by herself. Because she complained so much, her peers rejected her and her children rarely came to see her.

While she initially rejected the help of Ms. N, the social worker, the latter planned *not* to stop trying to make contact with her. The first part of the treatment plan took many weeks to effect; Ms. N would come to visit Ms. Lyons, and the latter would tell her to leave. When Ms. N would not leave but instead asked Ms. Lyons why she persisted in rejecting her, Ms. Lyons was eventually able to face that what she was doing to Ms. N was what she felt everybody was doing to her—isolating her.

When Ms. Lyons could acknowledge some of her own revenge, she became more comfortable in her therapy. She was able to pour out much anger and hurt, and as a result she became less desperate. She began forming some friendships in the institution and started to read to some of the blind senior residents. When Ms. Lyons was more comfortable with Ms. N and with her peers, the treatment plan shifted to an examination of the dynamics of Ms. Lyons's past and present relationships.

It is, of course, important to recognize that the notion of life-tasks is but one piece of data, albeit a crucial piece of data, that guides the clinician in planning treatment. Idiosyncratic history, current familial relationships, topographical, structural, and dynamic dimensions of the personality, and a host of other variables that we have discussed in this and preceding chapters are all pertinent to planning intervention.

In using the concept of life-tasks, it is crucial to remember that although two clients may be dealing with the same developmental conflict, each always has unique situational and personality strengths and limitations in coping with it. It should also be remembered that a client may have more than one life-task which causes conflict. Therefore, client and therapist have to decide which task deserves priority, what is more amenable to intervention, and what kind of environmental supports are available to the client for a specific life-task's resolution.

INDICATIONS AND CONTRAINDICATIONS
IN THE USE OF TREATMENT MODALITIES

In this chapter we have briefly referred to various treatment modalities: one-to-one long-term treatment, family treatment, group treatment, and so on. In formulating a treatment plan, client and therapist have to make a choice as to which modality or modalities will best serve the client. All clients and therapists have their biases and preferences, and it is hoped that these subjective investments will not unduly affect a plan that ideally suits the client. All too often, clients and therapists adapt to each other's preferences without thinking through carefully enough which modality will best enhance the client's psychosocial functioning.

Let us briefly consider some of the advantages and disadvantages of different modalities for different types of clients.

FAMILY THERAPY

In 1922, Mary Richmond pointed out that "the concern of the social worker is all those who share a common table" (Richmond, 1922). Social workers and other mental health professionals, since then, have recognized that modifications in one family member's coping style will almost always have a positive or negative impact on other family members. Clinicians have come to view the family as a dynamic system with interacting and transacting partners, all of whom contribute to the family's functioning and dysfunctioning.

Family therapists who treat the family as a unit—that is, all members are present for therapeutic interviews—point out that this form of treatment can help locate the family's "most burdensome problem" as all the members experience it (Pollak, 1956). Family therapists in their work try to expose each family member's responsibility for the continuance and maintenance of the system's "most burdensome problem." They have shown how communication, mutual understanding, and clarification of role discomplementarities can be enhanced when family members can look at themselves with each other in the "here and now" (Ackerman, 1958).

In family therapy there tends to be "shared blame" (Lidz, 1963; Pollak, 1958) so that family members are less likely to feel that they must carry the burden of the family's difficulties by themselves. They can learn that all problems are really shared—there are no saints and there are no sinners.

By locating how and when family members fail to express what they feel toward one another and how they misunderstand one another, the therapist can eventually help their interaction become smoother. "Double-bind" communication can be exposed, and neurotic accommodations can be pinpointed (Wynne, 1958).

In the Morton family, there were continual arguments between mother, father, sister, and brother. As Mr. A, the family therapist, watched with the members when and how the arguments would emerge in the family therapy, it turned out that almost all of them occurred when one of the members was feeling warmly toward another. The Mortons, albeit unconsciously, had made a family pact in which warmth and sexuality were to be repudiated and coldness and hostility were to be championed. As the Mortons could discuss in family therapy what they all feared about warmth, closeness, and sexuality, their arguments tended to diminish.

Ackerman (1958) has pointed out that when family members consider one another's problems in family therapy, the heightened feeling of "groupness" brings the family's concerns, conflicts, strengths, and limitations to center stage. The defensive maneuvers of the family, whereby the members support one another "to obscure the identity of the person who is the source of destructive reactions," also become apparent.

In working with families, family therapists have advised that interventions should be directed to the family as a whole. As the therapist focuses on patterns of interactions in the family and as all members learn to participate in the exchange with the therapist, they can eventually supplant the therapist's role (Leader, 1967).

Family therapy, like many other therapeutic modalities, tends to be too easily endorsed or too easily repudiated, depending on clinicians' preferences and prejudices. To determine more objectively whether family therapy is the treatment of choice, one of the most important questions that the clinician should ask is, "Is the family at a level of psychosocial maturation such that its members can be aware of and be helped to share and resolve a common problem to which they all contribute?" A positive answer of this question implies that the family members have ego functions available to empathize with one another, communicate openly without excessive rancor, take some responsibility for maladaptive interactions, tolerate some frustration as they listen to and try to understand other family members, and are not excessively narcissistic.

It is sometimes overlooked that many families that confront clinicians have members who are so infantile and so narcissistic that they really do not have those ego capacities available to share, to communicate, to empathize, and so on. Often, they have to project their difficulties onto other family members. Clients functioning at this level should not be expected to participate in family treatment; these clients seem to need a one-to-one treatment relationship in which they have access to one therapist, a parental figure who gives them complete attention so that their more elementary life-tasks are given the intense concern that they deserve.

While families who have the aforementioned ego functions available seem to be the best candidates for family therapy, there are certain immature families for which this treatment may be the treatment of choice. For example, after assessing a family's patterns of interaction, the practitioner may conclude that a strong symbiotic network exists. When the ties that bind a family are so strong, albeit maladaptive, family therapy may be indicated, simply because any other form of treatment may be much too threatening to the members of the family.

In some families, the members have strong defenses against communication. From a theoretical point of view, as with symbiotic families, family therapy, at first blush, may appear to be the treatment of choice. However, the individuals involved may not be able to bear the anxiety of sharing; hence, a one-to-one relationship with the practitioner should probably be considered, at least initially.

Family therapists, in their desire to help family units, have at times overlooked some important and crucial dynamics of therapy. Concentrating on the here and now, they can ignore how parents recapitulate their own idiosyncratic pasts with their children and how they unconsciously experience their youngsters as siblings, parents, and projected parts of themselves. When the past is overlooked and unconscious wishes and defenses are given limited consideration, it is really impossible to be expert on the dynamics of day-to-day behavior (Strean, 1982).

CONJOINT MARITAL TREATMENT

Conjoint marital treatment attempts to treat the neurotic interaction between two individuals rather than treat the individuals themselves. Advocates of this approach point out that dysfunctional marriages are not so much the result of a neurotic collusion but of a lack of role complementarity and dysfunctional role expectations. In contrast to the position held by most of their psychodynamically oriented colleagues, they contend that neurotic people can and do make good marriages, while many healthy individuals maintain unhappy marriages. They believe that the psychological status of a marriage is determined less by the personality difficulties of each partner, but more by the way the two personalities interact (Eisenstein, 1956; Ackerman, 1958).

Therapists involved in conjoint marital therapy believe that in the conjoint format the underlying interpersonal dynamics usually become more readily apparent to the spouses because they have the opportunity to understand each other in greater depth and to develop more empathy for each other. In front of a neutral observer, marital partners have the opportunity to perceive each other more realistically, and the therapist has the opportunity to see how the partners distort each other's communications. According to Martin (1976), the therapist in conjoint therapy is better able to limit destructive behavior and to facilitate the development of the observing ego of each partner so as to enable both to test reality more effectively.

One of the distinct advantages of conjoint marital therapy is that the couple and therapist can see how the marital pair conjointly resist in the treatment situation. This can give them some insight into their mutual fears in the marriage.

Lloyd and Susan Norton, a couple in their early thirties, were in conjoint therapy because they both felt "the chemistry was missing" in their sexual and interpersonal interactions. At home and in their sessions with their therapist, Mr. B, they battled constantly and were in frequent power-struggles.

Although Lloyd and Susan came to their sessions on time and seemed to be cooperating with Mr. B, the latter noted that from time to time they would come fifteen or more minutes late to their interviews. When Mr. B noticed this pattern and shared it with them, clients and therapist were able to figure out that the Nortons came late to sessions after they had not been fighting with each other in the previous treatment session. Feeling warm toward each other and toward Mr. B frightened them. They had to spend much time in their conjoint therapy trying to understand what was dangerous to both of them when they felt warmly toward each other.

Some of the disadvantages of conjoint marital therapy are that most of the time the unconscious motives of the individuals cannot appear spontaneously; confidentiality is not assured, and therefore many individual secrets are not forthcoming. Because of the nature of the format, the couple can use it to discharge complaints without getting to the wishes and defenses that keep these complaints alive. A possibility in conjoint therapy is that the partners may unite with each other and project onto the therapist their negative feelings about authoritarian or omnipotent parents, and therefore can defeat the therapist's efforts to effect change (Meissner, 1978). With its emphasis on the here and now, conjoint therapy can ignore crucial dimensions of individual history that are important etiological factors in the marital conflicts.

Some advocates of conjoint marital therapy, like some advocates of family therapy, can also overlook the fact that to participate in this treatment requires reasonably strong egos in both partners. Husband and wife have to be able to identify with the other, empathize, tolerate frustration, cope with anxiety, share the therapist, and control acting out. Many clients who have marital problems do not possess these abilities and it would appear that conjoint marital therapy is contraindicated for them.

Conjoint therapy seems to be the treatment of choice for those couples who have many ego functions intact, can communicate well with each other, and want to share and can share the therapist without experiencing too much sibling rivalry. These clients should be able to share secrets with their partners in a way that is not disruptive to their marriage or to their treatment.

WORK WITH SMALL GROUPS

Our society has become increasingly technological and impersonal. It may be that the growth of group therapy and group counseling represents a correction against the social isolation that many of our clients continually experience (Corsini, 1964). Groups satisfy the basic human need to belong—what Slavson (1943) has termed "social hunger." According to Tropp (1968, p. 267), the group

> is not only an alliance through which normal needs can be met; it can also be a natural healer of hurts, a supporter of strengths, and a clarifier of problems. It may serve as a sounding board for expressions of anxiety, hostility, or guilt. It often turns out that group members learn that others in the group have similar feelings weighing them down in their aloneness, that they are not so different or so alone—and learning this in live confrontation with one's peers is a most powerful change-inducing experience.

Group treatment, like family therapy, is a here-and-now experience, with the group experienced by its members as a symbolic family. In the group the individual member repeats patterns of interaction that he learned in his original family. As he interacts with "siblings," in the "here and now" he learns what he typically does to alienate and isolate others and also what he does and can do to bring others closer to him.

> Larry Olsen, age 11, was referred to a child guidance clinic because he was doing poorly in school, had no friends, and seemed quite depressed. His parents recognized that he was very much disliked by his peers but felt that this was because Larry's peers were immature. Larry seemed to hold a similar point of view.
>
> In an activity group, Larry was able to see for the first time that he had an arrogant and contemptuous attitude toward the others. As therapist and group members helped Larry see that it was actually Larry, himself, that did the rejecting, Larry eventually realized that he was treating others the way he felt his parents and brothers treated him—with derision and with contempt.

The decision to choose a group for a client would seem to have indications and contraindications similar to those of family treatment. A group may be very enriching and serve as a stimulant to maturer psychosocial functioning for children and adults who are very dependent on parental figures but who possess some impulse control and some capacity to relate to others empathically. Group therapy with children, for example, has been best utilized by the child who fears being autonomous in a social or educational setting but who can emerge as less socially anxious with peers with the practitioner's direction and interaction (Slavson, 1943). However, for a child or an adult whose capacity for interpersonal relationships is weak and who has never experienced intimacy and warm empathy from at least one parental figure, the group may be overwhelming.

Groups have been quite effective for clients who have the capacity to see themselves in a person-situation constellation similar to that with which others are coping. Mothers or fathers who can experience themselves emotionally as parents have profited from parents' guidance and other educational and therapeutic groups (Strean, 1970). However, ego-fragmented parents with strong, unfulfilled childish wishes often experience a discussion of parents' responsibilities as too threatening and respond with rage and depression—which suggests that a group is contraindicated for them.

The use of groups seems to be best indicated for clients whose major difficulties lie in their social and interpersonal relationships. In a group, they can examine their interactions with peers and locate which forms of interaction lead to conflictful and estranged relationships. This modality, to be helpful, seems to require in the client some ability to identify with others, empathize, and have impulse control and frustration tolerance; for clients who have not developed these capacities to any appreciable degree, one-to-one treatment would seem indicated.

Clinicians have noted that some clients who feel frightened and threatened by the intimacy of a one-to-one treatment relationship often welcome a group in which they do not have to expose themselves as much and do not feel so vulnerable. Here, the group can serve as a preparatory medium for other forms of help.

CRISIS INTERVENTION AND SHORT-TERM TREATMENT

With greater understanding of ego psychology, particularly notions of psychosocial tasks and the maturational timetable (Erikson, 1950), clinicians have been better able to understand the inevitable stress that accompanies living in our society. We now recognize that school entry, the death of a loved one, physical illness, pregnancy, and other important life events may induce a period of regression and overwhelming anxiety, but that frequently the client suffering from the effects of these events responds to help and returns to his or her previous state of equilibrium in a short period of time (Golan, 1978; Parad, 1965; Wolberg, 1968).

The principal goals toward which short-term treatment and crisis intervention are directed are: modification or removal of symptoms and relief of suffering; revival of the level of adaptive functioning that the client possessed prior to the crisis; promotion of the client's understanding of the most obvious problems that sponsor symptoms, sabotage functioning, and interfere with a more complete enjoyment of life; presentation of ideas about how to recognize these problems at their inception and provision of some way of dealing with such problems (Wolberg, 1968).

Short-term work seems to be the treatment of choice when the client has many ego functions intact, is not motivated for or interested in long-term treatment, and is not completely overwhelmed by the crisis.

> Mary Pearson, age 54, had a good relationship with her husband, who died suddenly of a heart attack. She had depended on her husband, Sam, in many ways: "financially," "emotionally," "sexually," and as "Mr. Fix-it." When she felt helpless and hopeless and told her family doctor about her distress since Sam's death, he referred her to a family agency.

> When Mary first met Ms. D, the social worker at the crisis center, Mary told her that since Sam had died, she felt like a helpless child. When Ms. D suggested that this was a common reaction to a sudden death of a loved one, Mary spent the remainder of the interview crying. During succeeding visits, as Mary found herself feeling warmly toward Ms. D, she shared with her how much she enjoyed feeling like a daughter to Sam and how, now that Sam was gone, she felt "like an orphan." Mary recalled in her third interview with Ms. D that her reaction to Sam's death was quite similar to the one she had had when her mother died. However, Mary recovered quickly when she "allowed others to mother her."

> When Mary realized how much Sam was "a good mother" to her, she started to reach out to others and with success. After three months of work with Ms. D, and after she found a male friend, Mary decided to "try it on my own."

Before deciding on crisis intervention or short-term treatment, just as with other modalities, the practitioner must assess the client's defensive patterns. There are some clients who experience sustained help as burdensome, overwhelming, or threatening. These clients may find it quite comforting to know in advance that their defenses will be not attacked but supported and that contact with the helping professional can terminate in a short period of time. They may use the clinician as they wish during the short period, returning at a later point for a more prolonged relationship or for intermittent short dosages of help.

LONG-TERM INDIVIDUAL TREATMENT

Long-term individual treatment is the treatment of choice when individuals wish to look intensively at themselves and resolve chronic symptoms and maladaptive interpersonal problems. One of the distinct advantages of one-to-one long-term treatment is that clients have the complete attention on themselves and can afford to look at fantasies, feelings, and memories in depth. One-to-one long-term treatment also has the distinction of providing an atmosphere whereby unconscious wishes, unconscious defenses, and unconscious superego injunctions can become conscious and worked through. In the one-to-one transference relationship, clients usually have a better opportunity to note how they recapitulate their problems in the here and now, and also to see how their current problems are repetitions of their history. Furthermore, in individual treatment, clients have the unique opportunity to assume responsibility for their own personal growth and change (Meissner, 1978).

As we have suggested, certain clients shun one-to-one treatment and this should always be respected. Short-term treatment should be the treatment of choice when the client very much wants it or is frightened of long-term work. Group therapy, dyadic treatment, and family therapy, as we have already indicated, are the treatments of choice in specified instances.

REFERENCES

Ackerman, N. (1958). *The psychodynamics of family life*. New York: Basic Books.

Austin, L. (1958). Dynamics and treatment of the client with anxiety hysteria. In H. J. Parad (Ed.), *Ego psychology and dynamic casework*. New York: Family Services Association of America.

Corsini, R. (1964). *Methods of group psychotherapy*. Chicago: William James Press.

Eisenstein, V. (1956). Sexual problems in marriage. In V. Eisenstein (Ed.), *Neurotic interaction in marriage*. New York: Basic Books.

Erikson, E. (1950). *Childhood and society*. New York: Norton.

Fine, R. (1981). *The psychoanalytic vision*. New York: Free Press.

Golan, N. (1978). *Treatment in crisis situations*. New York: Free Press.

Hamilton, G. (1951). *Theory and practice of social casework*. New York: Columbia University Press.

Hellenbrand, S. (1961). Client value orientations: Implications for diagnosis and treatment. *Social Casework, 42*(8).

Leader, A. (1967). Current and future issues in family therapy. *Social Service Review, 39*.

Lidz, T. (1963). *The family and human adaptation*. New York: International Universities Press.

Martin, P. (1976). *A marital therapy manual.* New York: Brunner/Mazel.

Meissner, W. (1978). The conceptualization of marriage and family dynamics from a psychoanalytic perspective. In T. Paolino and B. McCrady (Eds.), *Marriage and marital therapy.* New York: Brunner/Mazel.

Parad, H. (1965). *Crisis intervention.* New York: Family Services Association of America.

Perlman, R., & Gurin, A. (1972). *Community organization and social planning.* New York: John Wiley.

Pollak, O. (1956). *Integrating sociological and psychoanalytic concepts.* New York: Russell Sage Foundation.

Richmond, M. (1922). *What is social casework?* New York: Russell Sage Foundation.

Richmond, M. (1917). *Social diagnosis.* New York: Russell Sage Foundation.

Ripple, L., Alexander, E., & Polemis, B. (1964). *Motivation, capacity, and opportunity* (Social Service Monographs). Chicago: University of Chicago Press.

Slavson, S. (1943). *An introduction to group therapy.* New York: Commonwealth Fund.

Strean, H. (1982). *Controversy in psychotherapy.* Metuchen, NJ: Scarecrow Press.

Strean, H. (1978). *Clinical social work.* New York: Free Press.

Strean, H. (1970). *New approaches in child guidance.* Metuchen, NJ: Scarecrow Press.

Tropp, E. (1968). The group in life and social work. *Social Casework, 49.*

Wolberg, L. (1968). Short-term psychotherapy. In J. Marmor (Ed.), *Modern psychoanalysis.* New York: Basic Books.

Wynne, L. (1958). Pseudomutuality in the family relations of schizophrenics. *Psychiatry, 21.*

Chapter 4

THE CLIENT-THERAPIST RELATIONSHIP

The successful outcome of any therapeutic encounter is very much dependent on the nature of the client-therapist relationship. Regardless of how brilliant a therapist sounds, regardless of how empathetic he or she feels, and regardless of how accurate, timely, and appropriate his or her interventions are, if the client feels misunderstood, unsafe, or resentful toward the practitioner, the therapist's interventions will be rejected. There is virtually no client who has felt warmly and positively toward the therapist and who has left treatment prematurely. By the same token, virtually no client terminates treatment successfully unless he or she has felt that the therapist was a humane, interested, and helpful person.

Clinicians sometimes underestimate the importance of the fact that how their interpretations, confrontations, questions, and other interventions are received by the client has much more to do with how the client *experiences* the clinician than with almost any other variable. If a client is feeling negatively toward the therapist, the most astute statement or the most benign activity will be opposed; if the client feels positively toward the therapist, an incorrect statement or ill-timed activity will probably be endorsed, and if the client is ambivalent toward the therapist, almost everything the therapist says or does will be responded to with mixed feelings.

Not only is the successful outcome of treatment heavily dependent on the client's subjective feelings toward the clinician, but as we have already implied, the success or failure of therapy is very much influenced by how the therapist feels toward the client. If a therapist feels warmly disposed toward the client, there is a much better chance for the therapy to be successful than if the therapist feels negative or ambivalent. Therapists can distort their clients' behavior in the same way that clients can distort theirs. Each actor in the therapeutic drama brings his or her biases, fears, loves, and hates to the encounter, and these factors color all of their therapeutic interchanges.

Inasmuch as clients distort therapists' messages and therapists do the same with their clients, these two phenomena, transference and countertransference, need to be vigilantly observed throughout the helping process. The therapist frequently has to help clients see how and why they experience the therapist the way they do, and therapists need to study by themselves and/or with colleagues and supervisors their own countertransference reactions.

Because transference and countertransference are such crucial variables in all therapy—regardless of setting or modality of treatment—they require detailed discussion.

TRANSFERENCE

Anyone who has done therapeutic work has recognized that in the face of all logic and reason, the client may often behave in a most obstinate manner. Therapeutic progress is always influenced by the client's transference—the feelings, wishes, fears, and defenses that govern the client's perceptions of the therapist. Transference reactions are unconscious attempts by the client to recapitulate with the therapist types of interpersonal interaction similar to those experienced with significant others in the past. As much as some professionals would like to believe otherwise, clinicians are always perceived not only in terms of how they objectively are, but also in terms of how clients wish them to be and fear they might be. When therapists accept transference as a therapeutic given, they are not surprised when they are abhorred for trivialities or highly esteemed for banalities.

Freud (1925) singled out the notion of transference for much discussion. He pointed out that it is a universal phenomenon of the human mind and dominates the whole of each person's relations to the human environment. Transference, he further suggested, exists in all human relationships: in marriage, in the classroom, in business, and in friendships. Because of our unique histories, ego functioning, superego mandates, values, defenses, and social circumstances, each of us brings to every relationship wishes, fears, anxieties, and hopes that have evolved from previous relationships. Because these universal phenomena are essentially unconscious, we cannot will them away or quickly modify them. They influence our reactions, interactions, and transactions in every interpersonal relationship. Often we love or hate someone but cannot explain why. Usually the reaction is a transference response, which in therapy must always be studied and understood.

The intimate relationship of client and therapist is one in which the client depends on the therapist. This reactivates feelings that the client experienced toward others on whom he or she depended in the past. If the client experienced those who nurtured, guided, and educated him or her as essentially positive, the client will probably experience the therapist in the same way. However, virtually every client in the world, perhaps every person in the world, has residual feelings of love, hate, and ambivalence toward parents and parental figures; consequently, the attentive and sensitive therapist recognizes that he or she will be the recipient of all of these feelings.

THE EGO-IDEAL TRANSFERENCE

While transference reactions are usually traceable to childhood, there is not always a simple one-to-one correspondence between the past and the present. Frequently, there can be a compensatory fantasy to make up for what was lacking in childhood. In other words, the client fantasies that the therapist is somebody his mother of father should have been, that is, an ego-ideal.

> Roger Adams, age 26, after a couple of months of therapy, told his male therapist, Mr. Z, that the latter was "an ideal father figure." Mr. Z was described as "most kind, very supportive, and always knows the answers." Roger felt that ever since he had met Mr. Z, he was "walking on air."
>
> While Roger's idealized transference made his therapy very important to him, so that he could use it to his advantage, Mr. Z had to help Roger eventually understand that he was looking for an omnipotent parent. While he thought he had found this perfect parent in the form of Mr. Z, Roger needed to see that his perception of Mr. Z was in many ways based on childish wishes and childish fantasies.

When therapists recognize that transference always exists in all the relationships that clients have with them, they can look at their therapeutic results more objectively. If a client wants the therapist to be an omnipotent parent to whom the client can cling, then the client will fight therapeutic interventions aimed to liberate autonomy. If the client wants the therapist to be a sibling rival, then the client will use the therapist's interventions to maintain the sibling fight. Because the client views all of the therapist's interventions through the lens of his or her transference, the therapist must explore with the client not only why change is being resisted, but also, of equal importance, why the client wants to perceive the therapist in a childish way.

THE NEGATIVE TRANSFERENCE

Inasmuch as all clients have had less than perfect parents, they will inevitably feel hostile toward the therapist. Just as clients feel deprived by their parents, they will feel angry at their therapists for not loving them enough, not being sufficiently available, and not being sufficiently understanding. Furthermore, just as children resent their parents for having privileges and pleasures that they do not have, clients often feel angry because they are convinced that their position of "client" is an inferior one to that of the therapist.

A negative transference that is sometimes baffling to therapists is one that covers up positive and warm feelings toward the therapist. Many, if not most, clients are frightened of intimacy and love. When they feel warmly toward the therapist, they can unwittingly provoke a fight.

June Baker, a 24-year-old graduate student, was in therapy with Dr. Y because of depression, feelings of depersonalization, and an inability to sustain relationships with men. After a few weeks of treatment, June began to feel less depressed and more energetic. However, her cooperative demeanor toward Dr. Y changed and she became provocative and critical of him. When Dr. Y suggested that it might be a good idea to explore what had transpired between them that had made June's attitude shift, June was eventually able to recognize that to love Dr. Y made her feel "like a weak, helpless, kid." She further pointed out, "When I like you, you seem too big and I feel too small."

THE ID TRANSFERENCE

Clients frequently project parts of themselves which they find unacceptable onto the therapist. Frequently id wishes of a sexual or aggressive nature which are usually unconscious get projected. To ward off sexual fantasies, the client may accuse the therapist of being a dirty old man or a dirty old woman, and to avoid facing aggressive fantasies, the client may accuse the therapist of being a pompous ass or a condescending snob.

Marge Condon, 36, was in treatment with Ms. W for marital conflicts. She was a very inhibited woman who avoided spontaneity and was very constricted in her sexual behavior. When Ms. W suggested to Marge that it might be a good idea to explore why she had to deprive herself of pleasure, Marge became extremely angry. Fearful of looking at her own id wishes, she projected them onto Ms. W and told her that she seemed like a "depraved" woman who had many affairs and was very "irreligious." Inasmuch as Ms. W neither confirmed nor denied Marge's fantasies about her, Marge was eventually able to identify with the therapist's nondefensive attitude and face some of her own repressed sexual fantasies.

As was true in the above case, when clients project unacceptable parts of themselves onto the therapist, it is very important that the therapist neither deny nor confirm the truth of these perceptions. What the therapist should do is to give the client plenty of latitude to consider how and why the therapist is the kind of person the client perceives him or her to be. As the client is met with acceptance rather than with argument, the client is usually able to recognize eventually that what is observed in the therapist is being warded off by himself or herself.

THE SUPEREGO TRANSFERENCE

Most frequently clients project their own superego admonitions onto the therapist and expect the therapist to criticize them. Virtually all clients experience guilt about their real or imagined misdeeds and are sometimes quite convinced that the therapist, like the parents of their past, will censure them.

Because the superego is formed in interaction with significant individuals, it can be modified only through a corrective emotional experience with the therapist. As the client projects his or her superego onto the therapist, a consistent comparison of this projection with how the therapist behaves will serve to break down the punitiveness of the superego in the course of time (Fine, 1982).

Don and Estelle David, a couple in their late twenties, were referred for marriage counseling by a judge because they were engaged in physical brawls with each other. Projecting their superegos onto Mr. V, the social worker, they were reluctant to talk to him because they were convinced he would report them to the judge who would imprison them. It took many months for the Davids to accept the fact that Mr. V was not a person who was a judge, but a therapist who wanted to help them understand how upset they were and what their distress was all about.

Whatever the dynamics of transference are—projection of superego mandates, id wishes, or some other dimension of the client's psyche—a therapeutic relationship is distinguished from other relationships, not by these dynamics but by their place in the relationship, that is, the therapist's attitude toward the transference manifestations and the use that he or she makes of it. When a client seeks out punishment, criticism, or reassurance, in contrast to a parent or friend, the therapist wants to explore with the client what the client is experiencing that prompts these behaviors.

In dealing with a client's transference reactions, it is extremely important for the therapist not to question their validity, but rather to help the client see why he or she is looking for the type of reaction he or she is trying to induce. As Brenner (1976) has pointed out, a measure of scolding or a dash of encouragement may seem to hasten the therapeutic process. It can even, at times, produce symptomatic improvement. However, it is no substitute for an exploration of why the client wants to be admonished, punished, or praised. As Brenner (1976, p. 109) concludes, "In the long run it cannot fail to interfere to a greater or lesser degree with progress and with the achievement of an optimal end result."

IS THERE A CLIENT
WITHOUT A TRANSFERENCE?

Transference exists in all relationships. There is no such phenomenon as a client who has "no transference" or in whom transference fails to develop. When clinicians find themselves rejecting the fact that a client has transference feelings, they are rejecting part of the client's psychological reality.

There are clients, however, who do relate to the therapy as if the therapist were not present and seem as if they are not feeling even a modicum of love, hate, dependency, or ambivalence toward him or her. What the clinician should recognize in these situations is that the client is frightened to face certain transference reactions. He or she is denying them without a conscious recognition of doing so.

Pam Eagleton, a college student of 18, was referred to the student mental health center because of various somatic complaints, such as gastrointestinal problems, headaches, and insomnia. In addition, she was quite depressed and found it difficult to concentrate on her studies.

Although she willingly came to see her therapist, Ms. U, on a weekly basis, in her interviews Pam consistently communicated superficially about items such as the weather, the books she was required to read, or a movie she had attended. When Ms. U saw that Pam refrained from talking about other people in her sessions and asked her about this, Pam said that she did not have much to do with others. Eventually Ms. U could call Pam's attention to the fact that she was having little to do with her in the interviews. While Pam denied this interpretation for quite some time, eventually she was able to acknowledge that she was afraid to depend on Ms. U or on anyone else. Because she was very fearful of deep dependency yearnings which she had to deny and repress, Pam had to avoid Ms. U in the sessions and claim that she had no feelings toward her.

THE EROTIC TRANSFERENCE

The erotic transference, like any other transference, can have many possible meanings. As we have pointed out several times, behavior by itself does not tell us very much. One has to get to know the person quite well before the meaning of his or her behavior is clear.

An erotic transference can be a bid for reassurance, a defense against hostility, a substitute for a strong oral hunger, or a combination of several of these motives. When a client expresses wishes to see the therapist extratherapeutically and / or wants to know more about his or her life or more about the therapist's own feelings, thoughts, and fantasies, this usually heralds the beginning of an erotic transference. Sometimes a client will make a direct pass at the therapist and suggest they have dinner together or have some other form of rendezvous away from the office.

Working with an erotic transference requires much patience and skill. Many therapists become so anxious when they are sought after sexually that they change the subject or make interpretations which stop the flow of the client's material . As we will discuss in more detail later in this chapter, when a clinician observes a dearth of sexual fantasies in the client's productions, it may very well be that the therapist is subtly rejecting its expression.

If a client has a desire to be with the therapist sexually in or out of the therapist's office, what is important for the client to feel is that his or her sexual wishes will not be censured or criticized but will be understood in depth. It is hardly ever necessary to tell a client, "No, I won't go to bed with you," or "No, I won't go out with you on a date," but it is almost always necessary to tell a client, "Let's see what you are feeling and thinking when you want to go to bed with me or go out on a date with me." The message that the client should receive is that his or her fantasies are extremely important to examine and that therapist and client should understand what is *really* wanted by the client.

An investigation of the client's sexual fantasies in an atmosphere of safety and noncondemnation frequently leads to a discovery of infantile wishes that the client least suspected in himself or herself. The following vignettes illustrate this:

Dora Frank, a woman of 32, was in treatment with Dr. T. Dora had marital problems, a lack of sexual desire, frequent temper tantrums, and severe conflicts with her children, whom she found very difficult to discipline.

During her sixth month of twice-a-week therapy, Dora told Dr. T that she thought he was very attractive, that she had been having many sexual fantasies about him, and that she would like to go out for dinner with him.

Dr. T asked Dora to picture what would happen between them if they did go out for dinner. After Dora described a candlelit dinner, dancing, and warm embraces between the two of them, she fantasied going to a hotel with Dr. T to have sex. While the sex was described as passionate and enjoyable, Dora in her fantasies became much bigger physically, while Dr. T became much smaller. Eventually Dora fantasied herself as gloating and feeling smug because she had "weakened" Dr. T by getting him off his "high horse."

Dora's erotic transference was really an expression of revenge toward men, in general, and toward her father and the therapist, in particular.

Tom Gregory, age 27, was in treatment with Ms S. He was unable to sustain relationships with women, had interpersonal difficulties on his job as a salesman, and frequently found himself sexually impotent.

During his fourth month of therapy, he asked Ms. S at the end of a session whether he could walk her to her car. Ms. S told Tom that she was not going to her car at the moment but that she would like to talk further with him in the next session about what he had been feeling toward her that prompted his wish.

In the next session, Tom told Ms. S that he had wanted to talk to her more and walking to her car would prolong the session. Tom went on to say that he was a very lonely man and that he wanted to see more of Ms. S. As Ms. S encouraged Tom to discuss his fantasies regarding what they would do together, Tom told Ms. S that he visualized the two of them talking a lot, eating a great deal, and hugging for hours at a time.

When Ms. S observed that Tom's fantasies about her consisted essentially of foreplay, she brought this to his attention. Soon after this, Tom talked about his lack of confidence in his sexual capacities, his past and present impotence, and his strong wish to have the woman "take over" in sex. When this last fantasy was further explored, Tom revealed an unconscious wish to be a woman.

Tom's erotic transference, upon exploration, revealed an unconscious homosexual wish, a wish to reverse roles with the woman.

Rhoda Hastings, a woman of 40, had strong erotic fantasies toward her therapist, Mr. R. She was so attracted to Mr. R that she would have to commit suicide if he did not leave his wife and come to live with her.

When Mr. R asked Rhoda what she pictured if Mr. R would leave his wife and come and live with her, Rhoda fantasied that Mr. R would be with her all of the time—he would stop seeing patients and everyone else, and just be with her.

Rhoda's erotic transference was an expression of her deep symbiotic yearnings and her wish to make Mr. R an omnipotent mother who would never leave her little infant.

In the management of the erotic transference, if the client is permitted to talk about sexual fantasies in a nonjudgmental atmosphere, guilt is reduced and the client usually goes on to enjoy sex, rather than need it like an addiction. Paradoxically, the client with an erotic transference usually has a lot of ambivalence toward sex, much like the compulsive smoker who has mixed feelings toward his or her smoking.

As we suggested in Chapter 2, when sexual difficulties are present, the client is having difficulty coping with childish sexual fantasies. Most often the erotic transference is a composite of childish wishes and childish guilts which have to be discussed in the therapy.

A word should be said about the consequences of gratifying the client's wish for sexual or social contact with the therapist. It turns the therapy into a love affair, thereby negating its long-term benefits. Also, when the therapeutic relationship turns into a love affair, like all love affairs it offers only short-term benefits but no lasting or deep inner change (Fine, 1982).

THE DEPENDENT TRANSFERENCE

The dependent transference is one of the most common transferences. Most clients yearn for a parental figure, and they often believe that the therapist is the omnipotent parent who can deliver them to the Garden of Eden. Manifestations of the dependent transference are requests for advice and reassurance, desires for phone contacts with the therapist, constant and pressing demands of the therapist in and out of the sessions, and continual complaints that the therapy is ineffective.

The client with the dependent transference is frightened to be autonomous and separate, usually experiencing maturity as an intensely hostile act. That is why these clients want to be reassured so often. They are so worried about who they have hurt or destroyed that they need constant reassurance that they are still accepted and loved. They do not want to make decisions, because, once again, they feel that independence is a contemptible act.

When therapists answer these clients' questions, gratify their requests for reassurance, or give advice, they are preventing them from growing up. Instead, they are infantilizing them and are concomitantly coping with their own unresolved problems in a nonprofessional manner. When clients fear being autonomous, assertive, or normally aggressive, their fears should emerge in the therapy so that they can understand and master them better. The following vignettes demonstrate this notion:

> Michael Ingersol, age 30, was a single man who was sexually celibate. He was extremely frightened of relationships and spent most of his time by himself. He suffered from a variety of somatic complaints such as headaches, backaches, and insomnia.
>
> In his treatment with Mr. P, Michael would ask questions regarding the therapist's motives, therapeutic procedures, and how to conduct his life better. When Mr. P continually asked Michael what he was feeling and thinking when he asked his questions, Michael became even more helpless and told Mr. P his condition was becoming worse. On seeing that Mr. P was not manipulated by his questions or threats, Michael released a great deal of hatred toward Mr. P.
>
> In Michael's case, his questions and requests represented a defensive form of behavior to ward off hostile fantasies.
>
> Sally Joseph, age 32, was a mother being seen by Ms. O, a social worker in a child guidance clinic. Finding it difficult to discipline her children, Sally frequently felt helpless with them. As a result, her youngsters exploited her and manipulated her.

In her session with Ms. O, Sally constantly asked questions of Ms. O about how to handle the children. When Ms. O responded to Sally's requests by trying to help Sally see what she was feeling that immobilized her with her children and seemed to be immobilizing her in the sessions with Ms. O, Sally began to cry and brought out her strong yearnings for a mother to comfort her and nurture her. However, Sally went on to describe how her own mother was always available to her as a child and made all of her decisions for her.

In Sally's case, her dependent transference was a strong protest against being a nurturing mother and a mature woman.

Barbara Knisely, age 40, was in treatment with Dr. N for sexual problems and marital conflicts. After a month of treatment, Barbara began to ask Dr. N questions about his life, particularly how he solved his marital problems with his own wife. When Barbara's state of mind when she asked questions of Dr. N was explored in treatment, Barbara began to reveal many sexual fantasies about Dr. N.

Barbara's questions were a disguised way of trying to seduce Dr. N.

To the therapist, the most conclusive evidence of transference is the variety of different reactions he or she gets to the same objective event. For example, if a therapist puts a new painting in the office, there will sometimes be as many unique reactions as there are people. The only explanation of this lies in the fact that all clients have their own unique transference responses which are based on their own unique life stories. They need to be understood in their therapy.

COUNTERTRANSFERENCE

Countertransference is the same dynamic phenomenon as transference, except that it refers to those unconscious wishes, defenses, anxieties, and fantasies of the therapist that interfere with his or her objective perception and mature treatment of the client. Frequently, the client represents for the therapist a person of the past onto whom feelings and wishes are displaced. Experienced clinicians have acknowledged that rarely does a client not remind them of somebody in their present or past (Fine, 1982).

The term "countertransference" was first used by Freud (1910, p. 141), in The Future Prospects of Psychoanalysis, in which he said,

We have become aware of the "countertransference" which arises in [the analyst] as a result of the patient's influence on his unconscious feelings,

and we are inclined to insist that he shall recognize this countertransference in himself and overcome it. . . . No psychoanalyst goes
further than his own complexes and internal resistances permit.

Most clinicians since Freud's time have concurred with the notion
that the therapist cannot help a client grow psychologically any further
than he or she, the therapist, has matured. For example, if a therapist
has unresolved problems connected with aggression, then the therapist
may need to placate or be ingratiating with a client. Similarly, if a
therapist is threatened by his or her own unconscious homosexual
feelings, then he or she may be unable to detect homosexual implications in a client's material (Sandler, 1973) or may perceive them where
they do not exist.

Just as clients who have problems with dependency or autonomy are
going to bring these conflicts into their transference relationships with
their therapists, therapists with these conflicts are going to bring them
into their relationships with their clients. As a result, they can be too
reassuring, too critical, or too withholding, depending on how they
characteristically cope with anxiety. Let us look at a variety of common
countertransference responses.

OVERIDENTIFICATION

Treatment usually proceeds well when the therapist likes the client. If
therapists do not really care for the clients they treat, this will be
reflected in their interventions and the client will sense it. While a
positive countertransference is a desirable attitude, like a positive
transference it must be studied carefully (Fine, 1982).

A temptation for many therapists is to love the client too much. When
this occurs, the client is not perceived accurately or treated objectively.
In his or her overidentification, the therapist supports clients against
their real or fantasied opponents, rather than helping them understand
their own contributions to their own interpersonal conflicts. Overidentification frequently takes place in working on marital and parent-child
conflicts when the therapist sides with one member of a dyad against the
other (Strean, 1979).

Jack Lawrence, age 39, was in marriage counseling with Ms. M. In
discussing his marital conflicts, Jack described his wife as "bossy,
domineering, and cruel," while he himself was "kind, warm, and conciliatory." Ms. M was taken in by Jack's presentations and failed to realize

that behind chronic marital complaints are unconscious wishes. She erroneously joined Jack in his attacks on his wife and justified her behavior by pointing out that she was trying to help Jack assert himself. What was overlooked in Jack's therapy by Ms. M was his passive-aggressive demeanor and his own passive wishes to be dominated.

Only when Ms. M recognized her own countertransference problems was she able to help Jack understand how he was both inviting and sustaining a sadomasochistic relationship with his wife.

Just as transference reactions can and usually are rationalized and legitimized, therapists usually do the same with their countertransference reactions. When therapists side with one spouse against the other or with one family member against the other, they present "good" reasons for doing so.

The Morton family was in family therapy with Mr. L because mother, father, and son Bob, age 11, were always fighting with one another. Although no member of the family was exempt from provoking and sustaining the battles, Mr. L consistently sided with Bob against his parents, pointing out constantly in the family sessions that mother and father "misunderstood" Bob and were not treating him "compassionately." As a result of Mr. L's interventions, Bob became more smug and more arrogant and the parents became more helpless. Consequently, the family left treatment prematurely, feeling disillusioned.

THE EROTiC COUNTERTRANSFERENCE

Just as it is a natural phenomenon for clients to have sexual fantasies about their therapists, it is equally natural for therapists to have erotic fantasies about their clients. Experienced clinicians realize that it is par for the course of treatment to feel attracted to their clients. They also know that the more therapists are able to experience a genuine liking for their clients, the more they are usually able to help them. Many therapists feel guilty when they have erotic feelings toward their clients. They worry that they will act out their fantasies, so they take the path of least resistance and deny them altogether. This creates a tremendous problem for their clients, who frequently feel rejectable anyway. When they feel the therapist's lack of responsiveness, their low self-esteem becomes even lower.

The psychoanalyst Harold Searles has pointed out that "even with schizophrenic women [sic]," it is vital to give them the feeling that they are realistically attractive to the therapist. He places particular emphasis on the therapist's freedom to feel sexual toward his clients:

> Since I began doing intensive psychotherapy I have found, time after time, that in the course of the work with every one of my patients who has progressed to, or very far, toward a thoroughgoing cure, I have experienced romantic and erotic desires to marry, and fantasies of being married to, the patient. (Searles, 1964, p. 284)

Even though it is undesirable for therapists to act out their attraction toward their clients, it is quite the opposite with their feelings. Some therapists who cannot accept their natural and real sexual feelings toward their clients, instead of actually denying their feelings, displace them onto other aspects of their clients' functioning and praise them for their "mature" functioning.

> Pauline Norton, age 30, was an attractive-looking mother being seen in a child guidance clinic by Mr. K. Mr. K was taken with Pauline, whom he described as "bright, physically winsome, cooperative, and verbal." He responded to almost every production of Pauline's with praise. If she talked about her children, Mr. K told her what a good job she was doing; if she talked about an argument with her husband, Mr. K. would tell her what a feminine woman she was and that it was too bad that her husband did not appreciate her enough; and if she had an altercation with a friend, he told her the friend did not appreciate her enough. While Pauline initially enjoyed Mr. K's laudatory remarks, she grew suspicious of them and told Mr. K he was only "seeing parts" of her. When Mr. K justified his behavior by saying that Pauline found it too difficult to accept the truth, Pauline quit treatment, feeling that Mr. K did not understand her very well.

A NEED TO BE OMNIPOTENT

Many therapists, perhaps most, become clinicians so that they can derive some unconscious gratification from being a perfect parent. Being a perfect parent to clients can be a way to be vicariously parented; as the client thrives while being nurtured, the therapist's self-esteem rises. While it is extremely helpful for therapists to want to nurture their clients, this wish has to be tempered. If not, they become dominated by rescue fantasies and obsessed with therapeutic ambitions.

One way that therapists can gratify unconscious omnipotent fantasies is to be overactive in the treatment encounter. They can reassure rather than explore; they can interpret rather than listen; they can give advice rather than help their clients figure out their own destiny; and they can praise and punish rather than permit their clients to make their own evaluations of their own behaviors, thoughts, and feelings.

As we have already suggested, when therapists take over the sessions, they are indirectly taking over their clients' lives. This, of course, squelches their clients' autonomy, weakens their clients' capacity to become decisive, and lowers their self-esteem. Although many clients frequently fantasy having an omnipotent parent in the form of a therapist and may initially welcome the therapist's abundance of interventions, gradually they begin to resent how small they feel and start making bids to leave the treatment situation.

> Tom and Betty O'Conner, a couple in their early thirties, were in marriage counseling with Ms. J. Ms. J liked the O'Conners very much and had high hopes for them. When Tom and Betty discussed their marital disputes, Ms. J was very quick to make interpretations and to offer much support. While the O'Conners initially welcomed Ms. J's approach, they grew tired of it. After a couple of months, they told Ms. J that she was acting like an "overprotective mother" and making them feel they were like small children when with her. On seeing that Tom and Betty were making legitimate criticisms, Ms. J modified her activity and became more quietly reflective. As a result, the O'Conners were able to show their real capacities and grew.

Another way that omnipotent fantasies can be expressed by therapists is to not permit clients to disagree with them. As we discussed earlier in this chapter, when clients are in a negative or ambivalent transference, they are going to oppose the therapist's interventions, regardless of how appropriate and timely they are. Sometimes therapists forget that if a client needs to dispute an interpretation or object to an environmental manipulation, arguing with the client will hardly ever help. If a client needs habitually to disagree with the therapist, the client's wish to argue needs to be explored. "Pointing out reality" or "showing the client that he or she is using poor judgment" may help a therapist win a debate, but he or she may lose a client.

Whenever therapists find themselves trying to correct their clients' perceptions of their clinical activity, they should stop and reflect on why they cannot tolerate dissent. They should also try to understand why they and/or the client might be unconsciously arranging a power struggle.

Burt Parsons, age 26, was in therapy with Mr. I because he had problems
with authority and frequently was fired from jobs. Soon after therapy
began, Burt started to come to his sessions late and had nothing much to
say to Mr. I. When Mr. I interpreted to Burt that he seemed to be
opposing Mr. I the same way he opposed other authorities, Burt sharply
disagreed with Mr. I's interpretation and told Mr. I that the latter didn't
know what he was talking about. Instead of letting Burt talk out his
disagreements, Mr. I argued with Burt about the correctness of his
interpretations. Burt and Mr. I became involved in a power struggle, and
when Burt left treatment prematurely, his exit line was, "You'd rather be
right than be President."

THE HOSTILE COUNTERTRANSFERENCE

Inasmuch as therapists are human beings, they, like their clients, have
wishes, anxieties, and defenses. Therefore, it is inevitable that their
vulnerabilities will be activated in the therapeutic situation and that they
will feel hostility toward some of their clients. It is often difficult for
therapists to acknowledge their angry feelings toward their clients,
because, in their profession, hostility is considered a liability. Frequently, hostile feelings in a therapist are denied and repressed, and they
manifest themselves in disguised and subtle forms.

If a therapist finds that he or she arrives late for appointments, feels
bored, is overtalkative or undertalkative, is busily advising or criticizing
the client, these are usually signs of latent hostility. Hostility in a
therapist can exist for the same reasons it exists in a client. The therapist
may feel competitive toward the client, unloved, uncertain, or inept.
Therapists can suffer from hurt narcissism, insufficient success, or a
variety of other possibilities. Two of the most common expressions of
disguised hostility are the use of the clinical diagnosis as a countertransference expression and alterations of therapeutic plans and techniques
(Fine, 1982).

When clients are distrustful, isolate themselves from relationships,
and are frightened of the helping person, it is quite understandable that
the therapist gets discouraged, questions his or her own skills, and feels
quite angry at the client who does not show any progress.

Donald Rather, age 26, was an army veteran who was hospitalized
because of hallucinations, delusions, paranoid reactions, and depression.
Every time a psychiatrist, psychologist, or social worker approached him,
he refused to talk. Feeling very discouraged and angry, the staff acted out

their anger by diagnosing Donald as an "incurable schizophrenic," placing him in the back ward of the hospital and giving him drugs and electric-shock therapy.

When Donald was assigned to a student social worker, the student, unfamiliar with diagnostic terminology and unready to foist an unfavorable prognosis on Donald, greeted him humanely. Rather than withdrawing when Donald said he did not want help, the student sat through silences, listened to his client's complaints, and was not perturbed by his paranoid accusations and grandiose plans. Donald began, although at first with reluctance, to discuss his history and examine his anxieties and terrors, and eventually he was able to leave the mental hospital and take a job.

In a research project conducted by the writer (Strean, 1976), it was demonstrated that first-year social work students, because of their humane approach and absence of hostility, can be more helpful than perhaps any other professional to patients in mental hospitals who have been clinically diagnosed as schizophrenic. Unperturbed by notions such as "diagnosis," "prognosis," and "impeded ego functions," they seem to be able to relate in comfort to very disturbed people.

When the client does not respond to questions, confrontations, environmental manipulations, or interpretations, there is a tendency to express hostility not only by using pejorative labels such as "unmotivated," "hard to reach," or "psychopath," but also by applying "innovative procedures." These procedures, when examined carefully, often turn out to be sadistic attacks. Drugs, shock therapy, and backward isolation are administered when the patient or client rejects the therapist's efforts to talk to him. Sometimes the negative countertransference is expressed through verbal procedures.

Sue Smith, a 40-year-old mother being seen at a child guidance clinic, on many occasions refused to take the therapist's advice regarding child rearing. The therapist, Ms. A, responded to her own frustration by calling Sue "severely masochistic" and, under the guise of trying "to liberate her assertiveness," began to insult her. When Sue said that she was disgusted with her therapeutic progress (which was a muffled attack on Ms. A), the therapist told Sue that she was not a very good candidate for therapy. Rather than asserting herself, Sue became more depressed and more desperate and eventually left treatment.

There are a great many instances in which the therapist, because of unconscious hostility toward the client and/or toward supervisors and others, insists that the client is untreatable and resorts to all kinds of measures that make the situation worse. When therapists find themselves flirting with "special" or "innovative" techniques, they should first examine themselves to see if they are really quite angry at the client.

As therapists contribute to the growth of another human being, they should also experience growth within themselves. As Reuben Fine (1982, p. 212) has stated: "It becomes desirable for therapists to reformulate their conception of their role so that they look upon the entire therapeutic process as something that contributes to their growth as well as to that of the [client]". This can occur when therapists continually examine, understand, and learn to master their countertransference reactions.

REFERENCES

Brenner, C. (1976). *Psychoanalytic technique and psychic conflict*. New York: International Universities Press.

Fine, R. (1982). *The healing of the mind*. (2nd ed.). New York: Free Press.

Freud, S. (1925). *An autobiographical study*. London: Hogarth Press.

Freud, S. (1910). *The future prospects of psychoanalytic therapy*. London: Hogarth Press.

Sandler, J. (1973). *The patient and the analyst*. New York: International Universities Press.

Searles, H. (1964). *Collected papers on schizophrenia and related subjects*. New York: International Universities Press.

Strean, H. (1979). *Psychoanalytic theory and social work practice*. New York: Free Press.

Strean, H. (1976). *Crucial issues in psychotherapy*. Metuchen, NJ: Scarecrow Press.

Chapter 5

THERAPEUTIC PROCEDURES

In conducting psychotherapy, it is necessary for the therapist to specify what procedures are necessary to help the client at a specific phase of treatment. As we have stated several times throughout this manual, a therapist's good intentions, humane heart, and empathetic attitudes are indispensable for the success of treatment; however, they must be complemented by a comprehensive assessment and an individualized treatment plan.

As we discussed in Chapter 4, to implement the treatment plan, the therapist must be sensitive to the subtleties and intricacies of transference and countertransference. To help the client further resolve his or her conflicts, therapists must have an armamentarium of treatment procedures at their disposal. What therapeutic procedures are necessary to utilize in order to effect sound and humane treatment?

We suggested in Chapter 1 that one of the primary tasks of the therapist is to listen. As the client produces material, themes emerge and the therapist asks questions so that persistent themes receive elaboration. As certain conflicts, maladaptive behaviors, and dysfunctional attitudes of the client become clearer to the therapist, the latter confronts the client with them. For example, the therapist may draw attention to the client's persistent lateness to appointments and try to help the client recognize something that has been avoided in sessions heretofore. Usually confrontation is followed by clarification, which involves bringing psychological and interpersonal dynamics with which the client has been confronted, and which he or she is now more willing to consider, into sharper and more conscious focus. Clarification involves the unearthing of significant details from the past and the present that contribute to the etiology of the up-to-now uncovered phenomena (Greenson, 1967; Sandler, 1973; Fine, 1982; Strean, 1979). Interpretation of the dynamic meaning of the client's thoughts, feelings, and fantasies that emerge in the transference and in the client's daily life is a very significant part of dynamic psychotherapy. Its goal is insight, or self-understanding.

In social work and in other helping professions, the aforementioned procedures are sometimes accompanied by work in the environment, such as a school visit, a referral to a legal-aid society, or financial assistance (Hollis, 1972; Strean, 1978).

Working through is the integration of understanding by repeating and deepening insights and extending the meaning of the client's transference problems and other conflicts. Finally, the client synthesizes the insights by working out an adequate means of coping, in which anxieties are kept to a minimum and pleasure is derived from living.

Let us now examine some of these therapeutic procedures in more detail.

LISTENING AND ASKING QUESTIONS

In Chapter 1, we discussed the importance of both listening and asking appropriate questions. We pointed out that it usually takes many years of experience for a therapist to gain firm conviction that when a man, woman, or child is given an opportunity to verbalize thoughts, feelings, and memories to an attentive listener, tensions are reduced, understanding is achieved, mastery of conflict occurs, ego functions are strengthened, and psychic energy that had been used to repress and suppress disturbing thoughts and feelings becomes available for more productive living. When clients feel they are being regarded positively by a quiet and attentive listener, they begin to regard themselves more positively (Rogers, 1951). They tend to value themselves much more when the interviewer values what they say by listening to them carefully (Benjamin, 1974). Most interviewees sense when the interviewer is somewhere else, that is, when the interviewer is not listening fully; hence, silent listening without being attentive to the client's latent and manifest messages rarely achieves much therapeutic movement.

We also pointed out in Chapter 1 that an attentive listener should demonstrate that the essential points of the client's story have been grasped. The client usually feels heard if the interviewer, through pertinent questions (and later through confrontations, clarifications, and interpretations), illuminates significant features of the client's own accounts.

It was also emphasized in Chapter 1 that questions have to be phrased in unambiguous language so that they can be easily understood. Furthermore, when the clinician asks a question, there should always be a clear purpose in doing so. Perhaps more crucial than the exact formulation of a question is the attitude with which it is conveyed. The client should feel that the question evolves from the interviewer's empathy and identification with the interviewee. This helps the client, in most instance, to talk more freely and in increasingly greater depth.

CONFRONTATION

To help clients become more aware of the preconscious and unconscious feelings and thoughts that are contributing to their problems, the practitioner has to confront them from time to time with certain behavior of which they are unaware or only partially aware.

In confronting a client with a piece of his or her behavior, it is very important that the therapist has enough evidence available to support the confrontation. It is also crucial that the therapist have some assurance that the confrontation will be meaningful to the client. Premature demonstration of preconscious or unconscious material often compounds anxiety and only intensifies resistance to therapy.

Gerald Adler, a 19-year-old college sophomore, was in treatment with Ms. Z at a student mental health service at a university. During his first interview with Ms. Z, Gerald said in passing that Ms. Z was an attractive woman. He did not elaborate on this theme but mentioned it casually toward the end of the interview.

On arriving late for his second interview, Ms. Z immediately told Gerald that his lateness had something to do with his finding her attractive. Gerald protested and tried to change the subject. Ms. Z confronted him with his changing the subject and told him it was similar to his being late. She implied that when he felt anxious, he avoided the subject. While Gerald told Ms. Z that she "may have a point," he canceled his next interview and could not be persuaded to return for more therapy with Ms. Z.

The above vignette contains many lessons regarding how to confront a client. First, there should be ample evidence that the behavior is a crucial issue for the client. In the above example, evidence was sparse; there was only one lateness. Second, the interviewer should wait to see if the client has anything to say about the behavior in question.

Confronting a client at the beginning of an interview with an issue that is on the therapist's agenda and may be not on the client's is rarely helpful; it is more helpful to see what is on the client's mind before addressing the issue. Third, confrontations should take place after the therapist has done some thorough listening and has tried to ask a few questions; otherwise the confrontation appears too abrupt. Fourth, a confrontation is usually much more palatable to the client's psychic digestive system when a working relationship has been established between client and therapist. Most clients cannot ingest a confrontation when they are not confident of the therapist's "unconditional positive regard" (Rogers, 1951). Finally, as we pointed out in the previous chapter, arguing with a client about the correctness of a therapeutic procedure is never good practice.

To reiterate, it is extremely important when confronting a client to be sure that there is an ongoing working relationship between the actors, that there is enough evidence available to document the confrontation, and that the client has given some indication that he or she is ready to receive the confrontation.

> After three months of therapy with Janice B, a 34-year-old single woman, it became clear to Mr. Y, the therapist, that Janice canceled sessions following those in which she had expressed warm feelings toward him. After the cancellations had occurred several times, and after Janice had mentioned that she often found herself breaking dates with men without knowing why, Mr. Y asked Janice about her cancellations. He wondered if perhaps she was feeling some of the same discomfort with him that she did with other men when she broke dates. At first, Janice tried to change the subject. When Mr. Y remained silent, Janice said, "I guess I don't like to feel too close to any man." She later acknowledged, "I guess I don't feel comfortable when I like a male." Exploration revealed that Janice was afraid of closeness to a man because she was frightened of her sexual fantasies toward him.

In the above example, confronting Janice with her cancellations of appointments after she had shown some warm feelings toward the therapist enabled her to get in touch eventually with her sexual transference, which she feared. As she became a little more willing to consider some of the elements of her sexual transference, the therapist could then begin to help her clarify some of the meaning of her frightening sexual wishes.

CLARIFICATION

After clients have become more aware of wishes and thoughts, it becomes important for them to understand what fantasied gratifications frighten them and what impact these forbidden thoughts and feelings have on their lives. When clients have repressed wishes, fantasies, and ideas, they need to see what is dangerous about them if they were acknowledged consciously.

Janice, in the case example above, needed help in clarifying why she had to avoid her therapist and other men. By studying her transference reactions to the therapist, she slowly became aware of her fear of "falling in love with father figures." Janice was stimulated by and interested in her father sexually, but had to repudiate feelings toward him. She needed help in "digging out" significant details from her past that contributed to her resistance to men.

Clarifications frequently are meaningful and helpful to clients when they see that the behavior they are showing in the transference is similar if not identical to what is manifest in their daily lives.

Morton C, age 36, was in treatment with Ms. W because he had severe problems with authority figures. He battled repeatedly with bosses, landlords, and older colleagues. After Morton was continually provocative with Ms. W, and after he was confronted with this behavior a few times, he was later able to accept Ms. W's clarification when she said, "You feel that older people, like me, are contemptuous of you and you've got to fight back." Morton welcomed the statement and could give much documentation from his past and present to support it.

INTERPRETATION

After the therapist has listened to the client over time and has asked questions to illuminate certain themes, and after these themes have been confronted and clarified, interpretations are in order. Interpretation is that activity which helps the client become aware of the unconscious meaning, source, history, mode, or cause of a given psychic event (Greenson, 1967).

In the case of Janice B, discussed earlier, the therapist was able to interpret to Janice that she canceled appointments with him the same way she broke dates with men because she had to *punish* herself for her sexual feelings toward men whom she was making father figures.

With Morton C, also discussed earlier, the therapist was able to interpret that Morton needed to fight with figures of authority because he was afraid that he would be *dominated sexually*—much the same way he feared and wished to be dominated sexually by both of his parents.

The term "interpretation" is used in the psychotherapeutic literature to mean a variety of activities (Sandler, 1973):

(1) the therapist's inferences and conclusions regarding unconscious meaning and significance of the client's communications
(2) the communication by the therapist to the client of these inferences and conclusions
(3) all comments made by the therapist—confrontations, clarifications, questions, and so on
(4) verbal interventions specifically aimed at bringing about "dynamic change" through the medium of insight

As Sandler's summary suggests, the term "interpretation" has been used so frequently to refer to almost anything the therapist says that, at times, it seems too global. However, for purposes of discussion in this manual, we are referring to that activity which usually follows listening, questioning, confronting, and clarifying which, to repeat, is designed to make the client aware of the unconscious meaning of his or her attitudes and behavior. With this definition in mind, we can speak of three types of interpretation: uncovering, connective, and integrative (Fine, 1982).

THE UNCOVERING INTERPRETATION

The uncovering interpretation is one through which a concealed wish is brought to consciousness. Sometimes the wish is explicitly expressed in the client's statements and sometimes it is inferred by the therapist from the material. As we have implied, an inference presented to the client cannot be too far removed from his or her consciousness; otherwise, it will cause too much anxiety and/or be overlooked by the client.

Once a trusting relationship has been established between client and practitioner, the uncovering interpretation can be used quite frequently. It is probably the one that is used most frequently. The therapist is constantly attempting to help the client reduce anxiety, self-hatred, and maladaptive defensiveness and does this by trying to uncover sexual and aggressive fantasies so that the client can become more accepting of his or her human condition.

Mark Diamond, a 20-year-old unmarried man, was in treatment with Mr. V because he had poor interpersonal relationships, particularly with women. Mark either found himself secluded and socially isolated or involved in verbal fisticuffs. After about seven months of therapy, during which Mark both isolated himself from Mr. V and tried to argue with him, Mr. V made an interpretation to Mark that he was afraid to like him; consequently, he either fought with him or isolated himself from him. After several more confrontations and clarifications, during which Mark tried to fight or withdraw, he was able to report a fantasy that he had on the way to Mr. V's office. Mark fantasied that he and Mr. V were engaged in a warm conversation and then fantasized further that his fights and seclusiveness served as a defense against warm feelings, which made him feel very vulnerable.

Shirley Efros, a 22-year-old single woman, was extremely compliant in her interviews with Ms. U, as she was in all of her other interpersonal relationships. After several discussions of her present and past interpersonal relationships, Ms. U was able to interpret to Shirley that she needed her compliance as a defense to protect her against frightening aggressive fantasies.

In making interpretations, the therapist, in effect, tries to show the client how maladaptive defenses protect him or her against facing issues that provoke danger. In the case of Mark Diamond, his maladaptive defenses of isolation and fighting warded off the danger of facing warm feelings. In the case of Shirley Efros, her maladaptive defense of compliance warded off the danger of facing aggressive fantasies.

Interpretations, clarifications, and confrontations are, of course, utilized in all therapeutic modalities—short-term work, dyadic work, group treatment, and family treatment. However, when the unit of attention is more than one person, the clinician has to interpret (or clarify or confront) behavior and attitudes that the dyad, family, or group is utilizing as a system.

When the Frank family repeatedly came late for family sessions and when all the members consistently had avoided discussing feelings toward Ms. T, the family therapist, Ms. T was able to interpret to the family members that they were all afraid of revealing their feelings and thoughts to her. She apparently was experienced by all of them as a dangerous figure.

After a group of teenagers spent several group-therapy sessions blasting each other verbally and mocking the therapist, Mr. S, the group leader, was able to interpret to the group that they were all frightened of depending on one another and on the leader. Dependency seemed to frighten everybody in the group.

On seeing that John and Marsha Gregory continually focused in their marriage counseling sessions on their children and in-laws, Ms. R, the counselor, was able to interpret to them that they were frightened to look at their marital relationship with Ms. R. Having their ambivalent feelings toward each other exposed was very frightening to both of them.

THE CONNECTIVE INTERPRETATION

As was discussed in Chapter 2, all individuals are constantly experiencing the present as if it were the past. They frequently make relatives, friends, and colleagues into significant figures of their childhood. For example, many men unconsciously want their wives to be their mothers, their bosses to be their fathers, and their children to be their siblings. Women want their husbands to be fathers and can also distort who their children and colleagues are.

When a therapist makes a connective interpretation, the present is related to the past so that the client can see how he or she is distorting the present by waging old battles and seeking childish gratifications. When the client recognizes that the spouse is *not* the ominous parental figure of the past or that a colleague is *not* the dominating sibling of the past, anger usually diminishes and anxiety is dissipated.

Brian Halleck, age 40, was a father at a child guidance clinic because his son, Martin, age 10, had a severe school phobia. In discussing his own inability to release Martin and help him go to school, Brian was able to recall several incidents from his own childhood, when he had been Martin's age. One of Brian's memories involved a teacher who was very cruel toward children, particularly toward boys. Brian had many sadistic fantasies toward the teacher of his past and at times wanted to kill her.

Mr. P, the social worker who was treating Brian, was able, with the information that Brian supplied, to make a connective interpretation. He showed Brian that he was experiencing Martin as if Martin were the same 10-year-old that he had been many years ago. Mr. P also helped Brian see that he was misperceiving Martin's teacher by making her into the sadistic teacher of his own past.

Pearl Indik, age 40, was in marriage counseling with Ms. N. She found her husband, Herman, to be "a most intolerable man" and described him as "weak, ineffectual, and incompetent." After several months of therapeutic work, during which Pearl got in touch with a great deal of resentment and revenge toward her older brother, Ms. N could show Pearl how much of her rage toward Herman was a recapitulation of her old battles with her brother.

THE INTEGRATIVE INTERPRETATION

The integrative interpretation involves pulling together material from a variety of sources—from the past, from the present, and from the transference relationship. It is offered to help the client see his or her problems and life situation in a clearer perspective. Like all interpretations, integrative interpretations have to be repeated a number of times until the client is able to formulate a perspective in his or her own terms.

Phil Gold, age 37, sought treatment for sexual impotence, "homosexual panics" (fear that he would seduce men or boys), depression, and poor work habits. After a few months of treatment, during which he was quite euphoric, Phil became even more depressed than he had been when he initially sought treatment. His impotence returned, and he found going to work almost impossible.

One of the important etiological factors in Phil's life was that his father, to whom he had been very close, had died suddenly when Phil was ten. Phil, after his father's death, was in a constant rage toward his father for not being available to him.

Integrative interpretations helped Phil recognize that he was engaged in a futile battle with his father for not being with him all the time, and that this same fight was being relived in his transference relationship with his therapist, Mr. M. As Phil became more aware of the reasons for his wish to fight, he felt less depressed and more loving. Later he learned that he was using his compulsive aggressiveness to ward off loving feelings which frightened him.

ENVIRONMENTAL MODIFICATION

Although many therapists do not see modifying the client's environment as part of their clinical work, many clinicians, particularly social work clinicians, take the position that unless resources are provided or located for the client, and unless client needs are interpreted to influential persons in the client's social orbit, the client cannot be appreciably helped (Hollis, 1972).

As we suggested in earlier chapters, sometimes a therapist aggressively intervenes in a client's environment prematurely, and this is, of course, contraindicated. Furthermore, although there are many instances when therapists take over a task that the client can do by himself or herself, there are times when all of the talking in the world will not help the client, but an action of the therapist's will. For example, many clients need to be given food, clothing, and shelter before they can look at their psyches. Unless certain clients get some provisions to sleep, they are totally unable to talk about their conflicts to any clinician. The same can be said of certain medical conditions; until the client gets some medication or some other assistance from a physician, psychotherapy cannot be administered successfully, if at all.

Sometimes certain clients do not recognize that their environment is deficient in providing opportunities to find satisfaction for their essential strivings (Meier, 1965) and need help to locate a better job, physician, lawyer, and so on. Occasionally the clinician has to conceive of some of his or her work as that of "social broker" (Compton & Galaway, 1975) so that the client can be "hooked up" with a source of help that he or she can not secure alone (McPheeters & Ryan, 1971).

The Joseph family was referred to a family agency for marital problems, parent-child conflicts, and difficulties among the children. When it became clear to Ms. L, the social worker, that the family had not had a full meal for weeks, that there was no heat in their apartment, and that Mrs. Joseph had some serious physical ailments, these issues became paramount in the treatment plan, and the Josephs's marital and other interpersonal problems were given less priority until their more basic needs were satisfied.

As we will recall from Chapter 1, an individual, dyad, or family may resist environmental help. They may feel frightened to depend on the therapist, feel humiliated by the therapist because the latter is experienced as superior to them, or may believe that the role of "client" is one that is too overwhelming. When the practitioner notes that the client resists environmental help, he or she must determine what the danger is for the client.

On noting that Clara King had rejected the possibility of a new apartment, financial assistance, and medical help, the social worker, Ms. J, decided that she had to make Clara's reluctance to accept environmental help the focus of treatment for a while. On asking Clara what it was about accepting money, a new apartment, and the like, Ms. J learned from Clara that improving herself was tantamount to alienating herself from family and friends and that she "didn't want to be a snob." It took some time before Clara could resolve her feelings about being a snob, and during this time she could not accept anything from Ms. J.

INSIGHT, WORKING THROUGH, AND SYNTHESIS

As clients examine their pasts and current lives, as they look at fantasies, memories, thoughts, defenses, feelings, and interpersonal relationships, it is the goal of dynamic psychotherapy that, with the therapist's help (questions, confrontations, clarifications, interpretations, and possibly some environmental modifications), clients will achieve insight.

Insight is a dimension of psychotherapy that has been misunderstood. Some of the popular literature, as well as media such as film and television, have implied that one insight will heal a neurotic symptom (such as a phobia or a compulsion) or will heal a maladaptive form of interpersonal functioning. This never takes place. An insight has to be "worked through"—that is, elaborated, reviewed, and reconsidered—before it can have a real effect on the client's functioning. Insight, to be helpful in modifying disabling attitudes, neurotic symptoms, and dysfunctional interpersonal functioning, involves the lifting of repressions, the recovery of lost memories, the feeling of affects that were suppressed, and a new grasp of the significance and interrelationships of events (Schafer, 1977). Recollections take on a new meaning and the client may eventually say, "As a matter of fact, I've always known it, only I never thought of it" (Freud, 1914).

Sheer knowledge of defenses and of other sources of disturbance is ineffective in modifying emotional conflicts; otherwise, giving clients an article or a book to read would help them. Insight, to have an impact, always must be accompanied by genuine affect and real awareness in clients of how they have distorted their perceptions. Usually, when clients verbalize insights without functioning differently in any way, they are defending against the recall of a memory, repressing a fantasy or an idea, fighting certain feelings, or may be in a negative transference.

After the client comes to an insight—for example, understands that his disinterest in sex with his wife is because he is making her a mother of his past—the same interpretation has to be reviewed several times by client and therapist before the conflict ceases to be a problem. This is what is meant by "working through." It requires repetitive, progressive, and elaborate explorations of the client's fantasies, thoughts, feelings, and memories. As Greenson (1967, p. 42) has pointed out, "A variety of circular processes are set in motion by working through in which insight, memory, and behavior change influence each other."

If insights are worked through, there will be sustained change and symptoms, and maladaptive defenses will be given up. The therapist, however, should always remember that it takes time to integrate new ways of looking at attitudes, thoughts, and interpersonal behavior. The client characteristically moves two steps forward and one step back. The same issues, fears, and decisions must often be worked through over and over before clients can assimilate them and make them their own.

When maladaptive problems have subsided and insights are worked through, the client is ready to pursue love and work with enjoyment. Synthesis means that the client has worked out an adequate way of living, in which anxieties are kept at a minimum and pleasure from realistic ventures is at a maximum.

THE CLIENT'S RESPONSES TO
THE THERAPIST'S INTERVENTIONS

As we have already noted in this chapter and in earlier ones, when a therapist questions, confronts, clarifies, interprets, or intervenes in the client's environment, the client will respond to therapeutic procedures in his or her own idiosyncratic manner. The client's unique transference to the therapist and his or her unique dynamics are always going to influence how the client will respond. Experienced clinicians have frequently noted that the most carefully worded statement is not received by the client the way it was intended. A statement of support may be experienced as criticism, and a statement designed to challenge may be experienced as supportive. Even a simple question such as "Why not?" may be perceived as a command.

Bob Lord, age 29, in his first interview with his therapist, asked Mr. A, the therapist, if he thought he should switch his job. Mr. A, interested in exploring Bob's feelings about the job change, asked, "What do you suppose is in your way from switching jobs?" Bob presented several reasons that he could not take a new job. He was worried about changing his working hours, frightened of new demands on him, and concerned that his family might be deleteriously affected by the job change.

In Bob's second interview, he told Mr. A that he had taken a new job "because you told me to do so." When the therapist looked puzzled, Bob said, "Don't you remember? I said, 'Should I take the job?' and you seemed to say, 'Why not?' To me that meant that I should take it."

The client *always* experiences the therapist's activity or inactivity through the lens of the transference; hence, there is almost always something subjective and distorted in the client's response. Because the client inevitably attributes some unconscious meaning to the therapist's questions, confrontations, clarifications, and interpretations, therapists are often baffled at their client's responses to their interventions.

Ms. B was amazed that her client Sara Moody, age 27, always responded with anger to her interpretations that Sara felt lonely. When Ms. B regained her composure, she asked Sara about her angry responses. Apparently, every time Ms. B made an interpretation, Sara took it as a criticism.

Mr. C was baffled by his client Shirley Norton, age 22. Every time Mr. C asked questions of Shirley about how she was feeling about a particular issue, Shirley's face turned red and she became very silent. While it took a long time to find out, therapist and client eventually learned that Shirley experienced Mr. C's questions as sexual overtures.

In order to promote a productive helping relationship, therapists must observe, understand, and relate to the client's responses to their interventive acts. The decisive question with regard to the therapist's clarifications, confrontations, and so on is not whether a statement is correct but how the client reacts to it and what the therapist does with the client's reactions. On most occasions, therapists present the correct interpretation or perform the correct activity; yet their interventions may not bring about the results they strive for if they have not paid sufficient attention to how their words and actions are received and elaborated on by the client. Is the client listening to the therapist? Fully or partially? Is the client accepting the therapist's statement or rejecting it? Is the client ambivalent about it?

A client's verbal acceptance of the therapist's intervention is no proof that it is really being accepted. Some clients comply with the therapist's statements in the session but defy them when they leave. Certain clients may accept an interpretation out of a wish for love and reject one out of a desire to compete with the therapist. What is important is how the therapist responds to the client's rejection or acceptance of an intervention. The client may need help to see why he or she is compliant or may need to understand more about his or her competitive transference fantasies.

George Drake, age 17, balked at every one of Mr. E's statements, often calling him "a jerk, stupid, and a dirty old man." However, after demeaning Mr. E for a session or two, George would come in and tell Mr. E that he, George, "figured out the real story." With a few changes in words, George would repeat Mr. E's interpretations but call them his own. After this dynamic occurred several times, Mr. E could then confront George with his competition.

Therapy always consists of a dynamic dialogue. In the therapeutic encounter, the client's responses to interventions must always be subjected to careful study. The emphasis in dynamic psychotherapy is placed on the ways in which the client responds to interventions rather than on being solely concerned with their correctness.

REFERENCES

Benjamin, A. (1974). *The helping interview* (2nd ed.). Boston: Houghton Mifflin.

Compton, B., & Galaway, B. (1975). *Social work processes.* Homewood, IL: Irwin.

Fine, R. (1982). *The healing of the mind* (2nd ed.). New York: Free Press.

Freud, S. (1914). *Remembering, repeating, and working through.* London: Hogarth Press.

Greenson, R. (1967). *The technique and practice of psychoanalysis.* New York: International Universities Press.

Hollis, F. (1972). *Casework: A psychosocial therapy.* (2nd ed.). New York: Random House.

McPheeters, H., & Ryan, R. (1971). *A core of competence for baccalaureate social welfare and curricular implications.* Atlantic: Southern Regional Education Board.

Meier, E. (1965). Interactions between the person and his operational situations: A basis for classification in casework. *Social Casework, 46,* 9.

Rogers, C. (1951). *Client-oriented therapy.* Boston: Houghton Mifflin.

Sandler, J. (1973). *The patient and the analyst.* New York: International Universities Press.

Schafer, R. (1977). The interpretation of transference and the conditions for loving. *Journal of the American Psychoanalytic Association, 27*(7).

Strean, H. (1979). *Psychoanalytic theory and social work practice.* New York: Free Press.

Strean, H. (1978). *Clinical social work.* New York: Free Press.

Chapter 6

RESISTANCE AND COUNTERRESISTANCE

Throughout this manual we have frequently alluded to the client's resistive behavior and the therapist's counterresistive activity. In this chapter we want to examine these two phenomena in more detail.

Although individuals who are in psychotherapy invariably acknowledge that they are dissatisfied with the way they are coping with their interpersonal relationships, are disturbed by their neurotic symptoms, and are tortured by their low self-esteem, all clients unconsciously want to preserve the status quo, no matter how dysfunctional it is. Regardless of the setting and regardless of the modality, all clients present obstacles to their feeling and functioning better.

Inasmuch as most psychotherapists subscribe to the notion that the client's behavior, attitudes, and functioning are molded by unconscious and irrational motives, they are not dismayed when they observe clients arrive habitually late for interviews, cancel appointments, or denigrate the therapist. Therapists who accept resistance as an inevitable part of the therapuetic process are accustomed to hearing the sadistic spouse extol marital arguments as a way of life, the impotent man or frigid woman champion the virtues of celibacy, or the alcoholic client point out that his or her addiction is a sine qua non for life on earth. Because clients must protect themselves from the real and fantasied dangers that therapy induces, resistance seems to be an inevitable form of behavior in psychotherapy (Strean, 1985).

Just as the client's resistance seems to be a variable that is present from the beginning to the end of treatment, the therapist's counterresistance is consistently present. Therapists, out of their anxiety, can subtly and unwittingly squelch the expression of the client's anger, fail to confront the client on certain issues, find himself or herself frequently arriving late for interviews, or become bored and sleepy in therapeutic sessions. From the moment the client calls on the phone for a consultation to the termination of the contact, the therapist has fantasies and feelings toward the client that strongly influence the client's activity and inactivity in the therapy. Often therapists play a role in clients' absences from interviews, clients' tardiness, clients' nonpayment of fees, and other negative therapeutic reactions of clients (Langs, 1981).

When clients stop producing material and cease to examine themselves, we refer to this kind of behavior as *resistance*. Resistance is any action or attitude of the client's that impedes the course of therapeutic work. Inasmuch as every client, to some or to a large extent, fears self-examination and change, all therapy must be carried on in the face of some resistance. Resistance always implies that the client feels that some kind of *danger* is impending. As we have noted, individuals in therapy worry that they may be abandoned for their wishes, unloved for their assertions, attacked for their requests, or punished for their actions. When clients feel frightened about some impending danger, they have to protect themselves. What are referred to as defenses in the client's daily life (see Chapter 2)—projection, denial, repression, and so on—are resistances in psychotherapy. If, for example, a female client has a tendency to project her anger onto her husband and onto other individuals, in the therapy she will try to avoid examining her own angry thoughts and feelings and instead will report how her husband, friends, and relatives are hostile to her. She will also be inclined to accuse the therapist of being contemptuous toward her.

It is important to keep in mind that resistance is not created by the therapy. The therapeutic situation activates anxiety, and the client then uses habitual mechanisms to oppose the therapist and the therapy (Greenson, 1967).

When we discussed "assessment" in Chapter 2, we pointed out that the assessment will, in many ways, be a function of the clinician's view of personality functioning and his or her view of what is neurotic or maladaptive behavior. This same perspective has to be applied to the concept of resistance. For example, in a case illustration, ego psychologists Gertrude and Reuben Blanck (1979) pointed out that sending a postcard to a client during the therapist's absence helped the client with her sense of despair and depression. Upon returning to therapy, the client began arriving late for her sessions. The authors suggested that to regard the lateness as a resistance would have been damaging. Instead, the authors viewed it as an act of genuine and constructive independence. Psychoanalyst Robert Langs (1981, p. 463), in reflecting on the Blancks' material, stated that many therapists "would suspect that this behavior reflected a maladaptive resolution of underlying conflicts and fantasies, rather than a sign of true growth and independence."

Behavior such as lateness to appointments has different meanings to different clients because it emanates from different sets of motives, and as the above discussion suggests, the same behavior has different meaning to different therapists. From the therapist's perspective, the identification of resistive behavior relies in many ways upon the clinician's judgment, conception of maladaptive behavior, and notions regarding the dynamics of the therapeutic process.

TYPES OF RESISTANCE

Of the various attempts that have been made to classify resistances, the most thorough one and the one that has been used extensively by dynamically oriented therapists is Freud's 1926 classification, in his book *Inhibitions, Symptoms, and Anxiety.*

REPRESSION AND OTHER DEFENSES

In order to avoid a painful emotion, such as guilt or shame, that has been aroused by a forbidden sexual or aggressive impulse, the individual in therapy blocks the impulse from consciousness; that is, the individual *represses* the impulse. Alternatively, the client may *deny* the impulse and maintain that he or she feels nothing. The client could also *project* the forbidden impulse onto the therapist or onto someone else, such as a spouse or colleague.

The same client may use countless numbers of resistances in the same session or in several sessions.

George Anderson, age 30, found it difficult to acknowledge angry feelings toward Dr. Z, his therapist. In one session after another, he repressed his anger and said to Dr.Z, "Whenever I'm in your office, I feel nothing." Later he began to arrive for his sessions late, "forgot" to pay his bill, began to have his checks bounce, talked about how his family and friends questioned the value of psychotherapy, but concomitantly George denied that he had any angry feelings toward Dr. Z. Still later, George began to accuse the therapist of feeling angry toward him, thus projecting his forbidden wishes onto Dr. Z.

TRANSFERENCE RESISTANCE

Although Freud and many clinicians since his time have separated transference and resistance as two distinct concepts, transference must be viewed as a resistance because it preserves the status quo and protects the client against real or fantasied danger. When Freud initially conceptualized transference as a resistance, he pointed out that clients wish to perceive the therapist as if the therapist were a figure of the past, so that they can avoid facing unpleasant emotions and memories in the present. Rather than recognize their own wishes to continue a fight with parents or with other members of their family, clients frequently ascribe parental qualities to the therapist and then feel that the therapist is provocative, rejecting, and manipulative.

Transference and countertransference were discussed in detail in Chapter 4. It will be recalled that in that chapter we pointed out that if therapists do not understand how they are being experienced by their clients, they cannot be very helpful to them. We also stressed in Chapter 5 that all clients respond to their therapists' questions, clarifications, confrontations, interpretations, and environmental manipulations in terms of their transferences. If clients love their therapists, they will be inclined to accept most of their therapeutic interventions; if they hate their therapists, even the most neutral question, such as "How do you feel?" will be suspect. Finally, if they have mixed feelings, they will respond to most interventions ambivalently. Consequently, one of the major tasks of all clinicians is to be very vigilant in observing how their clients experience them and how they uniquely respond to therapeutic interventions.

EPINOSIC GAIN

A resistance that has been recognized by many practitioners for some time is the tendency for clients to derive unconscious gratification and protection from their neurotic symptoms. Although there is much conscious pain when the client suffers from a phobia, a compulsion, a psychosomatic disease, or a severe marital conflict, the client also enjoys the benefit of being relieved from responsibilities in work, marriage, or other areas of interpersonal life and therefore clings to his or her conflicts.

Inasmuch as a client can get considerable masochistic gratification from complaining about being the victim of a spouse's derision, an employer's belittling, or a bodily ache, the practitioner may unconsciously be perceived as an opponent who is trying to disrupt an important and needed psychological equilibrium.

> Nancy Bloom, age 39, was in marriage counseling with Ms. Y. Nancy spent all of her therapeutic hours severely criticizing her husband, David. When Ms. Y noted that Nancy had spent twelve years feeling miserable in her marriage and a year in therapy talking about her marital misery, she decided to confront Nancy with these facts. Nancy responded to Ms. Y with much anger. She said, "You don't appreciate how much of a victim I feel and you don't realize that divorce is impossible for me. I have to suffer."

The above vignette tends to substantiate the notion that a chronic marital complaint is an unconscious wish. Though Nancy Bloom was suffering in her marriage, the suffering protected her. In her case, she would rather have suffered than face the danger of being too intimate with her husband, David.

SUPEREGO RESISTANCE

In superego resistance, clients abuse themselves with guilt and self-punishment because of their unacceptable sexual and aggressive impulses. The discovery of superego resistance has helped many clinicians understand a frequent phenomenon in psychotherapy, namely, clients who give up maladaptive mechanisms, depressive conditions, and unhappy interpersonal interactions only later to start functioning worse and feeling horrible.

Superego resistance occurs when the client is unconsciously obeying a parental mandate never to enjoy pleasure; and/or when the client is in an unconscious battle with parents and others, and by getting better, he or she views the diminution of pain as a hostile triumph over the parents and others; and/or when the client, by feeling worse and functioning poorly, is unconsciously releasing anger toward the therapist and trying to defeat him or her. Superego resistance is always part of the negative therapeutic reaction, a phenomenon we will discuss at the end of this chapter. What is important for the therapist to keep in mind about superego resistance is that the client not only is punishing himself or herself but also is engaged in an unconscious battle with the therapist.

> After Mary Cambell, age 23, began to overcome a depression, started to date men, and felt quite elated, she became very depressed again.

Exploration revealed that she had to sabotage the efforts of her therapist Mr. V. As she concluded after several sessions, "When I get better, I worry that you feel too smug, and I can't stand that."

As we discussed in the chapter on transference, all clients during a great part of their therapy turn the practitioner into a parental figure. Many clients unconsciously try to take revenge on the therapist by not getting better, in the same way that they took revenge on parents by not functioning well in the outside world.

ID RESISTANCE

By the term "id resistance," we mean that type of behavior in which clients wish to receive gratification of unrealistic childish impulses, such as the wish to be omnipotent infants and have all of their childish demands met, pronto. Examples of id resistances are the client's wish to be the therapist's favorite client, making constant phone calls to the therapist, pleading for advice, and refusing to accept the frustrations that are necessary for therapeutic growth.

COUNTERRESISTANCE

All of the various types of resistance that have been enumerated can, of course, emerge as counterresistances in the therapist. Therapists can *repress* sexual or aggressive feelings that are being induced by the client; they can *project* their own irritation, sexual fantasies, or impotent feelings onto the client; or they can utilize a number of other defense mechanisms to protect themselves from their own anxiety in the therapeutic situation.

Ms. U, a therapist in private practice, was treating Richard Donovan, a man of 32, for sexual problems. Although Mr. Donovan was coming late for sessions, was canceling several, and was delinquent in paying his fees, Ms. U *denied* that this was a hostile expression on Richard's part. She was shocked when he quit treatment and only later realized that by denying Richard's hostility she was protecting herself from the danger of feeling rejected.

Mr. T, a social worker in a mental health center, was uncomfortable with his sexual fantasies toward Mary Erikson, his attractive 20-year-old client. To protect himself against the anxiety that evolved in his work with

Mary, he *projected* his sexual feelings onto her and constantly made interpretations that she was trying to seduce him.

The aforementioned examples could also be called countertransference reactions and are dynamically identical to the many examples of countertransference that we discussed in Chapter 4. Many therapists can gain satisfaction from keeping a client dependent by offering advice, praise, and criticism. They can also engage in power struggles that the client induces. Sometimes therapists can ignore latent transference wishes and resistive behavior of clients. All of these mechanisms can be a way for therapists to gain unconscious gratification and/or protection for their own neurotic problems. Therefore, therapists can derive *epinosic gains* from the therapy.

Dr. S was treating Jack Freedman, a 33-year-old passive, dependent, and sexually impotent man. Unaware that Jack's passive-dependent modus operandi threatened and irritated him, Dr. S was overactive and overinterpretive in the interviews. As a result, he unwittingly reinforced his client's problems and protected himself from experiencing his own.

Therapists, of course, can suffer from punitive superegos and can unwittingly squelch the client's verbalization of fantasies that are forbidden to the therapist. Some therapists are "unaware" of their clients' homosexual fantasies, others are unable to face their clients' rageful reactions toward them and toward significant others, and some therapists cannot tolerate their clients' dependency. When the therapist's superego is punitive, he or she cannot help clients truly express themselves, and the therapist's *superego resistance* interferes with therapeutic progress.

Ms. R, a therapist in a student counseling center at a university, was treating June Grant, a 19-year-old sophomore. In her interviews with Ms. R, June talked a great deal of her "sexual escapades." Unaware of the anxiety that provoked June's behavior and unaware of her own dislike of her own sexual fantasies, Ms. R told June to stop her sexual activity. Feeling misunderstood, June stopped her treatment, which, Ms. R later realized, she unconsciously wanted.

Just as a client can derive id gratification from maintaining childish ways of coping, the therapist can unwittingly derive vicarious gratification as the client acts out what the therapist would like to do. Just as the therapist's superego resistance interferes with the therapy, so does the therapist's *id resistance.*

> Mr. Q was treating Hank Halpern, age 36, for marital conflicts. Without realizing it, every time Hank talked about "telling off" his wife, Mr. Q found himself smiling. Mr. Q later realized that he "was having some fun" hearing how Hank's wife was being told off and was unwittingly encouraging him to do so.

Resistances have been categorized in different ways. Greenson (1967) has pointed out that the therapist not only should be aware of the source of the resistance (id, ego, or superego) but also should understand which aspect of psychosexual development is being resisted. Is the client fighting dependency wishes? Or is the client trying to ward off the wish to defecate and urinate all over the therapist? Possibly the client finds his or her Oedipal fantasies frightening? Furthermore, Greenson has advised that the therapist should clearly define the types of defense that are involved, such as isolation, undoing, or reaction formation. He or she should also be aware of the diagnostic category of the client—obsessive-compulsive, hysteria, and so on. Finally, Greenson points out that the therapist should determine whether the resistances are "ego-alien" or "ego-syntonic." Ego-alien resistances appear foreign, extraneous, and strange to the client's reasonable ego. An example would be when a client, for no apparent reason, feels that the therapist hates him and is about to throw him out of treatment. Ego-syntonic resistances are experienced as familiar, rational, and purposeful; they are usually habitual patterns of behavior, such as excessive compliance, marked orderliness, or extreme punctuality.

Reuben Fine (1982) divides resistances into those in which the client simply refuses, for one reason or another, to comply with basic requests and those in which the resistance is of a more subtle nature. Lateness, not talking, and refusing to pay fees are examples of the first category. More subtle are those resistances in which the client seems to be complying with basic requests but fights the therapy in one way or another. Examples of subtle resistances are an overemphasis on reality, a demand for gratification, a sense of hopelessness, or an absence of feeling.

Edward Glover (1955) divided resistances into two groups: obvious kinds of resistances and those that are essentially unobtrusive. Obvious resistances are "crass" and can scarcely be overlooked. The most obvious of all is when the client wants to terminate treatment. Other examples of obvious resistances are absences, latenesses, lagging on the way to the therapist's office, and delaying the departure from the therapist's office. Regarding unobtrusive resistances, Glover has referred to minor pauses, slips, inattentions, excessive compliance, and constant self-demeaning.

Leo Stone (1973) has discussed the ways transference can serve resistance: (1) resistance to the awareness of transference feelings; (2) resistance to the dynamic and genetic reductions of the transference—that is, reluctance of the client to see that transference feelings and fantasies are based on the client's idiosyncratic dynamics and unique history; and (3) resistance to giving up the transference attachment itself.

It is probably impossible to tabulate the various ways that resistance can be expressed. Any mental state (id, ego, or superego) or any defense mechanism can be pressed into the service of resistance. What is important for the therapist to recognize is that the same form of behavior in two different clients (for example, excessive compliance) can serve to protect the clients from different dangers. In one case the client might be protecting himself or herself from the expression of unacceptable and forbidden aggressive fantasies, while in another case the client is trying to ward off forbidden dependency wishes. It is also important for the therapist to determine the activity of the various psychic structures in the client's resistance. In the example of excessive compliance, the therapist should ask, "What superego mandates are being expressed, what defenses are operating, and what id wishes are being warded off?" The therapist should also be in touch with those aspects of the client's history that are being recapitulated. How was the client reared to make excessive compliance a modus operandi? Who reinforced this kind of behavior during the client's life? What are the fears that inhibit assertiveness? What is the current state of the transference?

In trying to help the client resolve resistances, the therapist should attempt to be "equidistant" (A. Freud, 1937) from the client's various psychic structures. By this we mean that the therapist does not try to persuade the client to give up the compliance, nor does the therapist attempt to persuade the client to maintain it. Rather, the therapist tries to show the client, by calling attention to the various structures in the client that are at work, why he or she is using a specific resistance. For example, an equidistant interpretation that maintains the therapist's neutrality would be, "You are frightened to express your anger at me because you were always told by your parents that this is forbidden. You are afraid I will retaliate the way they did." This equidistant interpretation neutrally presents to the client all of the psychic interpersonal issues that are at work. As we emphasized in Chapter 5, what will, of course, be crucial is the client's response to the interpretation. Does the client compliantly agree with the therapist? Does the client disagree? Does the client listen to the interpretation? What transference expressions evolve? Are there new resistances?

In resolving resistances, the therapist utilizes the same procedures that we discussed in the previous chapters. First the therapist listens to see what resistances emerge. Then questions are asked, followed by confrontations, clarifications, and interpretations. Therapeutic procedures to resolve resistances are no different from those used for any other part of treatment.

FORMS OF RESISTANCE

Let us now consider in more detail some typical forms of resistance in therapeutic work.

LATENESS

As we mentioned previously in this chapter and in earlier ones, behavior in and of itself does not tell us very much. A resistance such as lateness to appointments with the therapist can have different meanings for different clients, as the following two vignettes indicate.

Charles and Bessie Hyman, a couple in their mid-thirties, were being seen in marriage counseling by Mr. P. After four sessions with Mr. P, in which they were both very contemptuous of each other, they began to arrive late for their appointments. When Mr. P confronted the Hymans with their lateness, they denied that it had any meaning. However, when Mr. P, in a later interview, suggested that something about coming to see him was bothering both Charles and Bessie, which they preferred to avoid discussing, the Hymans began to move toward understanding their resistive behavior a bit better. It turned out that both Charles and Bessie were afraid to discuss their mutual criticisms any further, because "if it continues" said Charles, with Bessie agreeing, "we'll have to divorce and I'm not ready for that."

The Hymans' latenesses were an expression of their separation anxiety. Both of them were becoming frightened of their mutual hostility and were worried that continued expression of it would lead to a divorce.

Maxine and Harvey Itkin, a young couple in their twenties, were in marriage counseling with Ms. O. After about six sessions, which had been productive and helpful, the Itkins began to arrive late for their appointments. When Ms. O pointed out their latenesses to them, Harvey acknowledged that he was uncomfortable "about something" but was not sure what. Maxine took a similar stance. However, further exploration revealed that the Itkins were starting to feel closer to each other and both were becoming increasingly frightened about having sexual relations— something they both wanted to avoid. By coming late to their interviews, they gave themselves less of an opportunity to face the danger of looking at their sexual conflicts.

SILENCE

When clients resist by being silent, they are usually frightened about revealing some thought, feeling, or memory to the therapist. Often the client is apprehensive about what the practitioner will think of his or her angry, erotic, dependent feelings, fantasies, or behaviors. Like the child who anticipates punishment and hides from his parents, the frightened adult handles his or her anxiety through silence.

Mort Jackson, age 24, was in treatment with Mr. N. He was referred to Mr. N by a court judge because he had been involved in several thefts. In his interviews with Mr. N, Mort was silent for long periods of time. When he saw that Mr. N was not going to punish him for his silences but was only interested in understanding their meaning, Mort began to tell Mr. N how guilty he felt about his criminal offenses and how embarrassed he felt next to Mr. N, who appeared to be "an upright character." As Mort saw more clearly that he was projecting his own superego onto Mr. N, he could feel more relaxed with him and could reveal more to him.

Just as silence can be used as a resistance by a client, it can also be utilized as a counterresistance by a therapist. Therapists can muffle unacceptable sexual or aggressive feelings by silence. They can feel power over their clients through silence. They can detach themselves from an interpersonal relationship by being silent.

A single woman, Sheila Krill, age 28, was in treatment with Ms. M because she was not able to sustain relationships with men. In her interviews with Ms. M, Sheila spent most of the her time describing her passionate sexual affairs with men. Not consciously realizing that the interviews with Sheila were stimulating to Ms. M sexually, Ms. M handled her sexual anxiety by being very quiet. Eventually Sheila was able to detect anxiety in Ms. M, but when she mentioned it to Ms. M, the latter became even more silent. Sheila left treatment prematurely, feeling very much misunderstood.

RELUCTANCE TO PAY FEES

Inasmuch as money plays such a significant role in our society, inevitably it is used to express resistances in psychotherapy. Therapists and clients often resist having frank discussions about fees, and both usually have a lot of feeling about whether or not fees should be charged for missed appointments.

When clients are late in paying their fees, they are usually expressing some resentment about the treatment, the therapist, or the fee itself. Feelings of contempt or rivalry are often expressed through nonpayment of fees. Nonpayment of fees at times can also be an expression of sexual withholdingness.

It is always the therapist's responsibility to help clients understand what meaning money has for them—particularly when money, with all of its attendant affects and defenses, becomes an element in the therapeutic relationship. When clients use money to express their resistances, confrontation of the resistive behavior can help them function better, not only in situations that involve finances but in other interpersonal situations as well.

Larry Lyons, a 25-year-old saleman, was in treatment for ulcers and for other psychosomatic ailments. He was a very driven and competitive man who was in frequent arguments with colleagues, customers, and bosses. After he had been in treatment for about three months, he took off from therapy for a two-week vacation but did not discuss this in advance with Mr. J, his therapist. When he returned from his vacation, Larry insisted that he should not pay for his missed sessions because Mr. J "did not offer any service."

When Larry's behavior regarding his vacation was explored, he was able to tell Mr. J that he very much resented the latter's "controlling behavior" and "lofty position" and implied that he felt rivalry toward him. His vacation and refusal to pay the fee were his expressions of competition, contempt, and a desire to destroy the gains he had achieved in therapy.

As Larry discussed his competitive feelings and explored some of the dynamics of his competitive relationships in the past and the present, he began to realize how much pleasure he derived from weakening others. He also started to understand how his refusal to pay Mr. J was his way of expressing the kind of contempt that he experienced in most of his interpersonal relationships.

One thing that very much helped Larry in coping with his resistance is that Mr. J did not insist that Larry immediately pay the fee for the missed sessions. Rather, his attitude was, "More important is what you feel toward me when you don't want to pay the fee; let us understand that first."

THE CLIENT'S SITUATION AS A RESISTANCE

When clients seek therapeutic help, for their conflicted marriages, unsatisfactory job situations, poor relationships with the opposite sex, scholastic difficulties, or whatever, many, if not most of them, like to believe that they are victims of circumstance. Unhappy spouses blame each other for their misery; unhappy parents blame their children and vice versa; employers project their difficulties onto workers; and so on. Most individuals would rather believe that their unhappy situations are caused by forces outside themselves, and frequently they hope that they can enlist the therapist's support in ascribing blame to their marital partners, bosses, or others. Many of them want, and some demand, the therapist to manipulate their environments and change their spouse, boss, or teacher. However, it is of much more help to clients to learn how they are writing their own scripts.

> Boris and Polly Martin, a couple in their forties, and their children, Bill, age 12, and Shirley, age 10, were seen in family therapy because they constantly bickered, agreed on hardly anything, and seemed to receive limited pleasure from life, either individually or as a family.
>
> In their family therapy sessions, each of the Martins projected blame onto the others. Polly accused Boris of being too passive, Boris accused Polly of being too bossy, and Bill and Shirley complained that their parents demanded too much of them. Bill and Shirley also argued with each other a great deal.
>
> When Ms. I, the family therapist, confronted the Martins with her observation that they were resisting the family therapy by using the

sessions as verbal boxing matches, with each family member lashing out at the others, the meaning of this resistance slowly became clearer. Polly had to demean Boris because she had many sexual fears, and by criticizing him, she could keep him at a distance. Boris harbored a great deal of resentment that frightened him, and by being passive, he could control his hostility. Bill and Shirley could not face their deep yearnings for parental love and coped with their discomfort by arguing.

Although the Martins' critical statements about one another had some basis in reality, their functioning could not improve until each member of the family was helped to take some responsibility for the family altercations.

While it is often tempting for therapists to support their clients against a spouse, parent, boss, sibling, or teacher, clients will not feel better or function more maturely until they face and resolve their own contributions to their dysfunctional interpersonal interactions.

OVEREMPHASIS ON THE PAST

Just as clients can resist exploring themselves by focusing on others, they can avoid coping with the present by overemphasizing the past.

Adele North, age 47, was a divorced woman with many problems. She was at war with her children, fought intermittently with her ex-husband, was frequently in conflict with her colleagues at the school where she taught, was often in fights with her students, and was convinced the principal of the school was out to get her.

In her interviews, she focused almost exclusively on her past, damning her parents and her brother. When her therapist, Mr. H, pointed out to her that she avoided discussing her present circumstances but continually wanted to look at her past, Adele became furious. She told Mr. H that he was an unempathetic person who was oblivious to her suffering. Mr. H did not respond to Adele's hostility toward him, and in subsequent sessions she was eventually able to face the fact that she was yearning to be a little girl who would be taken care of by an indulgent mother. Talking about the past was Adele's way of keeping herself a child and avoiding adult responsibilities.

If the present is uncomfortable, as it was in the case of Adele North, the client may overemphasize the past. If fantasies and wishes arouse anxiety, the client may focus on superficial events of daily life. If the past is traumatic, the client may wish to discuss current issues, exclusively.

When there is an overemphasis on any aspect of the client's life, the therapist should always wonder about what is being concealed.

THE NEGATIVE THERAPEUTIC REACTION

Many clients cannot tolerate the state of feeling better and enjoying a more productive life. Each time they are successful, they feel guilty. When Freud (1923) discovered the negative therapeutic reaction, he referred to those many clients who could achieve insight into their problems, and accept their therapists' interpretations, but did not improve. No matter how much understanding they derived, their symptoms did not disappear, and in several cases they were exacerbated. Freud identified the force that prevented clients from utilizing their insights as the superego. He pointed out that clients with a negative therapeutic reaction punish themselves when they feel pleasure or experience success.

As we mentioned earlier in this chapter, contemporary clinicians recognize that clients with a punitive superego are also individuals with strong hostile fantasies. When they succeed at something, they unconsciously feel that they are destroying someone and for this expression of destructive wishes have to be punished. When these clients do not improve and maintain that they probably will never get better, it is important for practitioners to keep in mind that these clients are unconsciously directing their anger toward the therapist. In effect, the negative therapeutic reaction evolves because the client wants to defeat the therapist but feels guilty about his or her wishes to do so.

Bernard Ottinger, age 28, sought treatment because he was very depressed, felt horrible about his marriage, and disliked his job. After a few months of treatment, during which Bernard reviewed his past and present and seemed to make good use of the therapist's interventions, he pointed out to Mr. A, the therapist, that he had tried his best and was sure Mr. A had tried his best, but he, Bernard was sure that he was "just untreatable." When Mr. A asked Bernard how he thought Mr. A felt hearing this, Bernard imagined that Mr. A was probably feeling like a failure. Eventually, Mr. A could confront Bernard and later clarify with him that he enjoyed the idea of turning Mr. A into a failure, the same thing Bernard had wanted to with his father when he was a young boy.

As the discussions and case illustrations in this chapter imply, when individuals enter therapy, part of them unconsciously works against progress. All clients, regardless of how much they consciously desire their lives to be different and regardless of how much they are suffering, still fear change. Resistances are facts of therapeutic life, and understanding the reasons for their unique expression is crucial to both client and therapist.

REFERENCES

Blanck, G., & Blanck, R. (1979). *Ego psychology II: Psychoanalytic developmental psychology.* New York: Columbia University Press.

Fine, R. (1982). *The healing of the mind* (2nd ed.). New York: Free Press.

Freud, A. (1937). *The ego and the mechanisms of defense.* New York: International Universities Press.

Freud, S. (1926). *Inhibitions, symptoms, and anxiety.* London: Hogarth Press.

Glover, E. (1955). *The technique of psychoanalysis.* New York: International Universities Press.

Greenson, R. (1967). *The technique and practice of psychoanalysis.* New York: International Universities Press.

Langs, R. (1981). *Resistances and interventions.* New York: Jason Aronson.

Stone, L. (1973). On resistance to the psychoanalytic process. In B. Rubinstein (Ed.), *Psychoanalysis and contemporary science.* New York: Macmillan.

Strean, H. (1985). *Resolving resistances in psychotherapy.* New York: John Wiley.

Chapter 7

TERMINATION

Inasmuch as psychotherapy inevitably activates pain and anxiety, clients, as we have seen, constantly resist the process in direct and indirect ways. Some clients find the process so difficult that they end it prematurely, and some therapists find doing treatment with certain clients so unbearable that they, too, end the process prematurely. However, the majority of clients and therapists survive the various treatment crises that evolve during the treatment encounter and sooner or later have to face the issue of terminating the therapy.

The dynamics of termination have been neglected in the psychotherapy and social work literature, yet they constitute a dimension of the treatment encounter that all clients and practitioners must confront (Strean, 1985; Fox, Nelson, & Bolman, 1969). In most cases, clients have experienced the therapist as an empathic ally; consequently, separation from the therapist will not be a matter-of-fact phenomenon but, like any other human loss of importance, can generate a sense of helplessness and grief (Briar & Miller, 1971). Separation from the client can be discomforting for the therapist, as well. Therapists have an emotional investment in the process and in their clients' lives, and they, like their counterparts, are not immune to feelings of grief and loss.

Perhaps some of the neglect of the subject of termination in the psychotherapy literature stems from the fact that termination stirs up painful associations for both therapists and clients—memories of rejection, abandonment, and loss. As Fox, Nelson, and Bolman (1969) have suggested, the gap in the literature may be a reflection of the therapist's "defensive processes against the affects involved in termination—a sort of institutionalized repression."

As much as therapists and clients wish to avoid confronting the end of their relationship, as with every other issue of importance in the client's life, the feelings, memories, and ideas associated with separation must be expressed, understood, and mastered. If not, some of the gains of treatment may be lost, and clients will not receive the help they need in confronting future separations during the rest of their lives.

CRITERIA FOR TERMINATION

THE THERAPIST'S ORIENTATION

Many factors influence the decision for therapy to terminate. One of the criteria is the therapist's theoretical orientation to treatment. For example, if one is a behaviorist and looks solely at external behaviors, there is little problem. All one has to do is to determine if the client's symptoms have disappeared. Thus, behaviorists Briar and Miller (1971, pp. 168-169) state,

> a youngster who, for whatever reasons, is judged to be a problem because he will not attend school can be thought of as successfully treated when his school attendance becomes reasonably frequent. A child who suffers from enuresis is "cured" when he no longer wets himself. The case of an impotent man can be closed when he experiences erections. An unemployed father is satisfactorily treated when he obtains and holds gainful employment.

For those therapists who view the human being as a complex biological, psychological, and social organism, the disappearance of one symptom is an insufficient criterion for termination. Symptom eradication may not necessarily enhance a client's self-esteem, lessen guilt, reduce hatred, or touch many of the dimensions of the client's psychic life or interpersonal relationships. If the therapist believes that hopes, dreams, emotions, fantasies, and other internal states are significant, then these factors must be taken into account when considering termination.

Utilizing the psychosocial approach that has been emphasized throughout this manual, criteria for termination are much more complicated than is, for example, a behavioristic approach. Questions such as "Have the ego functions been enhanced?" "Has the superego been reduced in its punitiveness?" "Is the client more able to enjoy sex?"

"Has the client's capacity to love been increased?" should all be answered in the affirmative, providing, of course, that the client has been in treatment long enough for these possibilities to occur.

Regarding criteria for terminating psychotherapy, Freud (1917, p. 457) referred to the neurotic individual's "return to health" in terms of "whether the subject is left with a sufficient amount of capacity for enjoyment and of efficiency." Freud took the position that an individual is ready to terminate therapy when he or she can enjoy the realities and cope with the frustrations of work and love.

Most writers on the subject of termination agree that neurotic symptoms such as phobias, compulsions, and obsessions should have subsided and that the client should have some understanding about how and why symptoms evolved; otherwise, there is the risk of rearousal of symptomatology after termination (Dewald, 1972; Firestein, 1978; Jones, 1936).

A few writers have pointed out that the person terminating psychotherapy is not going to be exempt from conflict for the remainder of his or her life. Hartmann (1964, p. 6) has averred that "a healthy person must have the capacity to suffer and to be depressed." Aarons (1965), drawing on Hartmann's work, has pointed out that in successful psychotherapy conflicts are resolved, but not eliminated, and are replaced by a choice of alternatives.

A practical means of assessing a client's readiness to terminate psychotherapy is to determine how near he or she approximates "the analytic ideal" (Fine, 1982). This would mean that the client has reduced his or her hatred markedly and can love easily, is able to communicate with a wide range of feelings, is part of a family and of the society, can enjoy sex, is creative, and shows an absence of neurotic symptoms. In addition, the client's ability to separate from the therapist without too much anxiety is also implied in Fine's criteria for termination.

LENGTH AND FREQUENCY OF TREATMENT

If a client has been involved with a therapist for several years and for one or more interviews a week, reactions to separation from the therapist will probably be more acute than if the contact is of short duration, particularly if the short-term work was centered on specific services, such as the provision of a homemaker or referral to another agency or therapist. According to some of the proponents of short-term work, clients react well to termination in response to time limits that are agreed on early in the encounter. Furthermore, they have averred that when a termination date is set well in advance, clients seem to accelerate their progress (Reid & Epstein, 1972).

What has not always been sufficiently considered by practitioners involved in short-term therapy is that the constraints set up at the beginning of the treatment may not be conducive to helping clients feel that they have the right to express all they feel about termination. When clients have been told at the beginning of treatment that they will have only six or seven sessions to resolve their problems, it is difficult for them to raise questions and express resentment about a contract to which they concurred. In addition, the therapist doing short-term work, who is usually "task-oriented," may not always be sensitive to the many affects that clients harbor at termination.

> The Adams family was in short-term family therapy with Ms. Z because the Adams's son, Tom, age 10, had a school phobia. Although Tom returned to school before the six sessions of therapy were over, the Adams had other problems that were not addressed in treatment.
>
> In their later treatment contact with Ms. Y, which began two months after the previous therapy had terminated, the Adams told Ms. Y that they were very attached to Ms. Z, did not want that therapy to end but did not feel it was appropriate to say so. Mr. Adams also told Ms. Y that even after a "check-up" was made by Ms. Z "to see if everything was okay," he did not feel he could "honestly say how I felt."

If the therapist has not given sufficient concern to the client's situational pressures, psychological stresses, wishes, expectations, anxieties, resistance, and transference reactions, the client is likely to squelch his or her feelings about termination. Therefore, problems and issues that were left unattended will probably emerge after termination.

When a contact is brief—even when there have been only one or two interviews—clients can have feelings toward the therapist and can have difficulties about termination.

> Carl B, age 25, had a brief contact with a travelers' aid agency. Warmly received and empathically related to by the social worker, Ms. W, Carl had a lot of feelings about ending his contact with her. Accepting her money to go to Chicago from New York to find work, Carl returned to New York three weeks after he had seen Ms. W and said, "I missed you so much. I couldn't find anybody like you in Chicago. I'd rather be a bum in New York than a worker in Chicago."

Whether a therapeutic encounter consists of one or one hundred interviews, the practitioner frequently emerges as an important significant other, and separation will inevitably arouse complex and ambivalent feelings.

ATTAINMENT OF CLIENT GOALS

One of the reasons that termination and separation are sometimes an unsuccessful experience for clients is that the therapist failed to differentiate between task accomplishment and the termination of the relationship. Many clients have been able to improve their functioning and reach the goals they set for themselves at the beginning of treatment, but are not ready to leave the therapist. This was certainly true in the preceding two case vignettes. If the therapist is too goal-oriented, he or she may lose sight of the importance the client places on the treatment relationship. This does not mean that the therapist must ipso facto gratify the client's wish to prolong the contact. Rather, the therapist should explore the client's resistance to termination.

A mothers' group met with a social worker in a child guidance clinic for nearly a year, with the goals of improving their relationships with their children and of enhancing the day-to-day functioning of their children. Most of the mothers had accomplished the tasks they had set for themselves. However, when the social worker, Ms. V, suggested that the group be disbanded, the members protested. They all felt close to one another and close to Ms. V and wanted to continue the group sessions.

Inasmuch as Ms. V recognized that these mothers all had difficulty emotionally separating from their children, which was a throwback to unresolved problems in separating from their own mothers, she used this knowledge to help the group members discuss their fears of independence and anxiety about autonomy. After the group spent several sessions discussing their separation anxiety, they could accept the discontinuance of the group with more equanimity.

While some therapists have incorrectly utilized the client's goals as the sole basis for determining when termination is indicated, others have not been sufficiently attuned to what the client really needs from treatment—the subject of Chapter 3, "The Treatment Plan." Lack of a treatment plan may endlessly prolong the treatment; with no goals established, the client can maintain a dependent relationship that is not in his or her best interests.

Marilyn Diamond, age 23, had been in treatment with Mr. T for more than two years. She went into therapy because she was having interpersonal difficulties with men. Mr. T posited as his goal with Marilyn "a corrective emotional relationship with a benign father figure." Because his goal was so global, treatment went on and on, with both parties gratified to some extent by the relationship but with little effort expended by either party to help Marilyn with her fears of autonomy, assertion, and independence.

It is important in any discussion of termination for the therapist to remember that within a nebulous framework, as in the case of Marilyn Diamond, motivation to separate from the therapist and become more self-directing may never develop. If clients are not sure why they started treatment and continue the process, they are hardly ever in a good position to discuss its ending.

SEPARATION ANXIETY

As we suggested at the beginning of this chapter, if the client has found the therapist to be an empathic ally, separation will not be a matter-of-fact phenomenon but, as when the loss of any other important person is experienced, can generate a sense of helplessness and grief (Briar & Miller, 1971). Inasmuch as termination conjures up painful emotions, many clients regress and manifest the same symptoms and interpersonal problems that they presented at the beginning of treatment. By their regression, they are expressing a wish to begin treatment all over again instead of ending it. Annie Reich (1950) has suggested that revived symptoms and revived interpersonal problems form the client's reaction to the awareness that childish wishes are not going to be gratified by the therapist. Saul (1958) has concluded that the reappearance of old problems is an expression of revenge. The client, in effect, is saying, "See, you have had no impact on me."

It would appear that under the impact of separation, many clients are crying out for a parent to comfort them. In many ways, therefore, the anxiety that clients experience at termination can be likened to the way children feel at weaning. Having been the recipients of tenderness, love, and care, they are reluctant to give up a gratifying experience. While children and adults have an impulse to grow, they also resist the requirements of independence and autonomy. Their anger and/or depression at this time is an expression of protest at being weaned from the therapist's benign breasts.

Although all clients react to termination in their own idiosyncratic manner, no client is exempt from feeling separation anxiety. Even though clients can feel pleasure about a job well done, it is essential for the practitioner to recognize that every client who faces termination has to cope with frustration. Hopes and fantasies are punctured, and certain unique gratifications of being listened to and receiving unconditional positive regard from the therapist must be relinquished. That is why many clients at this time make derogatory remarks about the therapist and the therapist's procedures and become skeptical about professional help (Firestein, 1978).

> Sixteen-year-old Barry Fine had been in weekly treatment with Dr. S for about a year, and much progress had been made. Initially a withdrawn young man who was doing poorly in his schoolwork, Barry had begun to expand his social relationships and was doing much better in his schoolwork. When Barry began to show less conflict in all of his activities and had talked more about enjoying his independence, Dr. S asked Barry how he would feel about being more independent of him. After saying that he thought terminating the treatment was a good idea, within three weeks, Barry's schoolwork began to deteriorate and his interpersonal relationships became quite conflicted again. When Dr. S pointed out that Barry seemed to be responding with upset to the idea of terminating treatment, Barry became quite indignant. He told Dr. S that the latter was "a stupid shrink," "a money-hungry bastard," and "a dope."
>
> When Barry's hostile challenges were listened to without comment but with benign interest, Barry began to feel his loss and grief and told Dr. S that he was "an excellent therapist" and a "great father figure." After three or four weeks of talking about his loss, grief, and punctured fantasies, Barry moved the frequency of his therapy to every two weeks instead of once weekly. Even then, some of his longing persisted for another month or two before Barry could think again of some of the pleasures of being independent.

In reviewing the above case, it becomes apparent that even in short-term treatment on a weekly basis, the client can have strong resistances to termination. Barry, like many other clients, had to work through his strong wish for an attachment to a parental figure. In his termination phase, Barry regressed, his symptoms returned, and he felt acute anger. Consequently, many sessions were needed for Barry to resolve his separation anxiety.

When confronted by the client's regression and by the revival of symptoms, beginning therapists can feel quite upset. They start to wonder about their own competence, worry if they have had any impact at all on their client, and may even go as far as wondering whether psychotherapy can help anyone. These reactions, of course, mirror what many clients feel during the termination phase, and sometimes this is what clients would like their therapists to feel.

It is important for clinicians to recognize that termination inevitably provokes regression and anxiety in virtually every client, and clients need an opportunity to ventilate their anger, their fears, and their helplessness. When therapists view their clients' regression during the termination phase as inevitable, they are not so prone to knock themselves, lose confidence, and question the value of the psychotherapeutic process.

If clinicians do not recognize that anxiety is always present in their clients at termination, they will be inclined to falsely reassure their clients, respond angrily to them, or do something else that is antitherapeutic. What clients need more than anything else at termination is the freedom to regress, the opportunity to express anger, the right to feel helpless, and the permission to question the therapist's competence. When they are given these opportunities, they are usually able to organize themselves and eventually move on.

INDIVIDUALIZING SEPARATION

Termination and separation, like any other issue in psychotherapy, must be individualized for each client. If therapists have understood their clients well, they will be better able to anticipate their clients' reactions to termination. For example, if clients, during the course of their therapy have shown conflicts around "trust versus mistrust" (Erikson, 1950), they will probably distrust their own therapeutic gains and distrust the goodwill and competence of the therapist. If they have shown problems with autonomy, their doubts about it will assert themselves at termination. If initiative has been a problem for them, they will fear taking some. If they have shown problems on several levels of development during their therapy, all of these problems will, in all likelihood, manifest themselves at the end of treatment.

Sam Gold, age 37, had been in treatment with Ms. R for three years on a twice-weekly basis. He entered treatment because of sexual difficulties, inability to sustain relationships with women, and feelings of inferiority.

During the course of his treatment, strong Oedipal conflicts emerged. He frequently used Ms. R as the object of his fantasies and was able to feel much less guilty about his incestuous fantasies and competition with men.

As Sam was moving toward a more secure relationship with a woman, enjoying himself more sexually, and taking initiative with less conflict, he initiated the idea of termination of his therapy. While Ms. R remained neutral about the idea of termination, Sam felt sufficient confidence in himself to set a date for the end of treatment. For about two weeks he was feeling pleased with himself. However, slowly he began to feel depressed and began to denounce his therapy and question the value of it. When Ms. R did not respond to Sam's villifications, he was slowly able to bring out a fantasy that he harbored throughout his relationship with Ms. R. The fantasy was that he could have an affair with Ms. R.

Sam needed several months to discuss with Ms. R how angry he was to remain simply a client of Ms. R's and to bring out his frustration at never being her "one and only." His intense Oedipal conflict, which had been a predominant theme in his therapy, was also a central theme during termination.

Just as termination and separation mean different things to different clients, therapists have their own unique reactions, depending on the story of their own lives. Therapists usually find that different clients affect them differently. Some clients at termination will induce a wish to hold on to them; others will stir up a desire to let go. Some will stimulate a feeling of failure, and others will induce a feeling of success. Some clients will induce all of these reactions. As we suggested in Chapter 4, therapists must constantly study their own reactions and try their best to see that their countertransference responses do not affect their clients deleteriously.

Mr. P had worked with his client Joe Heming, age 30, for more than three years on a twice-weekly basis. Joe had made many gains in his therapy. He had reduced his clinging dependency, increased his self-esteem, and was much less hostile. When Joe and Mr. P discussed termination, Mr. P noted in himself a wish to "get rid of" Joe quickly. As he studied his wish, he realized he had been making Joe his younger brother, whom he had wanted to "get rid of" during his own childhood.

Although each client and each therapist will have unique responses to separation and termination, there are some common reactions. We have already discussed the ubiquity of loss, mourning, and grief. Many clients (and some therapists) feel guilty about success, viewing it as a hostile triumph, and this needs expression. Dependency conflicts frequently emerge, and, as we observed in the case of Sam Gold, certain omnipotent fantasies get punctured. All of these issues need careful exploration.

As fantasies of onmipotence are toned down, as dependency wishes are modulated, and as other resistances and counterresistances are resolved, client and therapist are ready to take leave of each other. However, therapeutic work continues after the formal ending because the client has learned a way to confront problems and to overcome anxieties.

REFERENCES

Aarons, Z. (1965). On analytic goals and criteria for termination. *Bulletin of the Philadelphia Association of Psychoanalysis, 15,* 97-109.

Briar, S., & Miller, H. (1971). *Problems and issues in social casework.* New York: Columbia University Press.

Dewald, P. (1972). The clinical assessment of structural change. *Journal of American Psychoanalytic Association, 20,* 302-324.

Erikson, E. (1950). *Childhood and society.* New York: Norton.

Fine, R. (1982). *The healing of the mind* (2nd ed.). New York: Free Press.

Firestein, S. (1978). *Termination in psychoanalysis.* New York: International Universities Press.

Fox, E., Nelson, M., & Bolman, W. (1969). The termination process: A neglected dimension in social work. *Social Work, 14*(4), 53-63.

Freud, S. (1917). *Analytic therapy.* London: Hogarth Press.

Hartmann, H. (1964). *Essays on ego psychology and the problem of adaptation.* New York: International Universities Press.

Jones, E. (1936). *Papers on psychoanalysis.* Boston: Beacon Press.

Reich, A. (1950). *Psychoanalytic contributions.* New York: International Universities Press.

Reid, W. & L. Epstein (1972). *Task oriented basework.* New York: Columbia University Press.

Saul, L. (1958). *Technique and practice of psychoanalysis.* Philadelphia: Lippincott.

Strean, H. (1985). *Resolving resistances in psychotherapy.* New York: John Wiley.

ABOUT THE AUTHOR

DR. HERBERT STREAN is Director of the New York Center for Psychoanalytic Training, and Distinguished Professor Emeritus, Rutgers University. He is the author of thirty books and over one hundred professional papers. Some of his popular books are *Behind the Couch, Resolving Resistances in Psychotherapy, Resolving Counterresistances in Psychotherapy, Our Wish to Kill, Resolving Marital Conflict, Jokes: Their Purpose and Meaning*, and *The Use of Humor in Psychotherapy*.

In his forty years of professional practice, Dr. Strean has trained over 4,000 therapists. He has been on the editorial board of *Psychoanalytic Review, Clinical Social Work*, and *Analytic Social Work*, and is currently Editor-in-Chief of *Current Issues in Psychoanalytic Practice*. Dr. Strean maintains a private practice in New York City.